Graham Jones is managing director of Top Performance Consulting Ltd. His experience of consulting with top-level perfor~~~~ ~~~~ ~~~~ ~~~~ ~~~~ and includes working closely with senior l~ and Fortune 500 companies. He has wo including World Champions and Olympi ranked performers from a wide variety of sp swimming, hockey, squash, judo, boxing, ic worked closely with the Royal Marines.

Formerly Reader in Sport Psychology at Loughborough University before becoming Professor of Elite Performance Psychology at the University of Wales, Bangor, Graham has more than 150 publications in the area of top performance. These include several books, numerous groundbreaking studies in scientific journals, and applied articles that demystify and unravel complex concepts and theories in performance psychology. His recent publications include the article, 'How the Best of the Best Get Better and Better', published in *Harvard Business Review*, and his fourth book, *Thrive On Pressure: Lead and Succeed When Times Get Tough*, published by McGraw-Hill.

Graham co-founded leading performance development consultancy, Lane4, in 1995 and has specialised in working with high-profile leaders and their teams. Graham left Lane4 to set up Top Performance Consulting Ltd (www. tpc.uk.net) in 2010, where he continues to work with leaders and their teams in large business organisations, as well as expanding his reach to charities and smaller organisations.

Some of the organisations he has worked with include Goldman Sachs, St Mary's Hospital in Paddington, Coca-Cola Enterprises, The Coca-Cola Company, J.P. Morgan, LinkedIn, HSBC, Blind Veterans UK, Roche Pharmaceuticals, UBS, DaimlerChrysler, Marie Stopes International, Sainsbury's, 3M, National Grid, Nationwide, Siemens Healthcare, British Airways, easyJet, Accenture, Otis Elevator Company, Deutsche Bank, Dyson, Ericsson and Fujitsu UK.

Also available from How To Books

Developing Mental Toughness
Gold medal strategies for transforming your business performance
Graham Jones and Adrian Moorhouse

A Practical Guide to Mentoring
How to help others achieve their goals
David Kay and Roger Hinds

Coaching Skills for Leaders in the Workplace
How to develop, motivate and get the best from your staff
Jackie Arnold

Managing Conflict in the Workplace
How to develop trust and understanding and manage disagreements
Shay and Margaret McConnon

Setting Up and Running Effective Staff Appraisals
and Feedback Review Meetings
How to set up an appraisal system that really will improve individual
performance and organisational results
Dr Nigel Hunt

TOP PERFORMANCE LEADERSHIP

Graham Jones

Constable & Robinson Ltd
55–56 Russell Square
London WC1B 4HP
www.constablerobinson.com

First published in the UK by How To Books,
an imprint of Constable & Robinson, 2014

A copy of the British Library Cataloguing in Publication Data
is available from the British Library

ISBN: 978-1-84528-573-9 (paperback)
ISBN: 978-1-84528-574-6 (ebook)

1 3 5 7 9 10 8 6 4 2

Printed and bound in the UK

For Tara. Thank you.

Contents

List of Illustrations

Acknowledgements

A big thank you to the following people for their contribution to making this happen:

- Dr Tara Jones for providing valuable input to the manuscript, as well as being a wonderful wife
- Jonathan Goldman, Graham Hodgkin, John Peters, Dom Sheldrick and Sue White for agreeing to participate as members of the Advisory Board and who have done such a great job
- Sam Lewin for 'doing' the bits of the manuscript that my own, very limited IT skills couldn't handle
- Mike Nelson for putting me right on airplane cockpit design (see Part 2)
- Nikki Read and Giles Lewis at Constable & Robinson for their support and for making my life as easy as possible from the publishing angle

Also, thank you to the anonymous people who were interviewed for the study that forms the foundation of some of the content in Part 4.

Introduction: Yet *Another* Book On Leadership!

So many leadership books, so few *real* leaders

There are thousands of books on leadership and I am conscious that this is yet another one in serious danger of being an unopened purchase or 'bookshelf filler' that seemed like a good idea at the time. At this point, at least I know you have opened it! But the threat to the book does not end here; it could be another unfinished read that got sidelined and eventually discarded because of other priorities and demands. So why should you finish reading this one? What difference will it make? Sadly, most books on leadership do not make a big difference to the leaders who read them, the evidence being quite simply that there are so few *real* leaders. Instead, there are many people in 'leader' roles who are ineffective because they do not know how to be a 'real' leader or they have no interest in putting themselves on the line and being a 'real' leader. So how will this book make a difference?

Who am I to talk about leadership?

It was more than a decade ago now but I recall the experience as if it happened yesterday; five amazing days that make the hairs rise on the back of my neck as I think about them.

It began on a Sunday in November when I was on a bus transporting the Wales rugby team to the Millennium Stadium in Cardiff. It had been raining all day and our police escort made slow but steady progress through the thousands of people milling about the city's streets in eager anticipation of what was about to unfold.

This was the culmination of an entire week's focus and preparation for a match against the then World Champions, Australia. A whole nation, starved of recent success, was watching closely and both players and management were intensely aware of the scrutiny they were under. I had run a couple of sessions with the team during the week and I had spent one-on-one time with players on things like composure, focus and belief. However, a lot of my time was also spent talking with members of the management. They knew that they were running out of goodwill from the governing body, the Wales Rugby Union, and were feeling the heat; a heavy defeat would be too much to bear. In the final moments before they left the changing room to walk out on to the pitch to be greeted by more than 70,000 noisy fans, I shook hands with the players and wished them well as I retreated with the management team to watch from a box high in the stands. There was no more the coaches could do but watch and hope the best-laid plans would be implemented and effective. Wales lost 21-13 but it was a close-run game and the team performed well against the world's number one.

Two days later, on the Tuesday, I was with the Board of Coca-Cola Enterprises UK, who produce, sell and deliver Coca-Cola products. A colleague, Dr Austin Swain, and I had been working with this team for some time as the result of an employee survey which highlighted a low level of confidence in the leadership team and a level of staff turnover above industry average despite good business performance[1]. The Board lacked cohesion, a long-term vision and supportive personal relationships, and it was clearly impacting on the employees. On this particular Tuesday, the team was faced with a serious business problem that had to be dealt with quickly and appropriately. This was the world's best-known brand

---

1 This information was made available in the public domain with the permission and collaboration of CCE UK in the form of a case study: G. Jones. 'Coaching high achievers', *Internal Communication*, May 2006, 17–18.

and I was fronting a session to help get them out of a hole. Happily, the meeting went well and it was pleasing to witness the work we had carried out over the previous months to develop them as a cohesive and supportive team come to fruition. We were able to have open and challenging, yet calm and trusting conversations that concluded in a solution that had everyone's buy-in and commitment. I walked away feeling relieved and extremely satisfied, knowing they had an effective plan to avert what could have been serious repercussions.

By the Thursday I had arrived at the Royal Marines Commando Training Centre in Lympstone, Devon. This is the principal military training centre for the Royal Marines and a colleague, Professor Lew Hardy, and myself had been called in to work with the sergeants who were responsible for training new recruits. Our remit was to help them deal with the high and rising attrition rates among recruits early in their training. The leadership needed guidance and support on how to adapt training methods that had been used since the Second World War to suit the 'new generation' of entrants without lowering the requisite physical and mental standards to be awarded the coveted 'Green Beret'. We met with the Commandant of the Training Centre on this particular day to gain an inside knowledge of the workings of one of the world's elite fighting forces and to agree the parameters of our intervention. Our work eventually culminated in quasi-experiments where sergeants who were trained by Lew and myself in specific leadership techniques had higher retention rates than their counterparts who did not receive the training[2].

This account of my 'five days' encapsulates so much about leadership that is applicable across all performance settings: the

---

2 L. Hardy, C. Arthur, G. Jones et al. 'The relationship between transformational leadership behaviours, psychological and training outcomes in elite military recruits', *The Leadership Quarterly*, 2010, 20–32.

pressure to succeed; the vulnerability that accompanies the inevitable visibility and exposure; the uncertainty that can excite or frighten; the responsibility to do what is right; the courage and commitment to change something that has worked in the past; the willingness to put the organisation before self-interest; the passion that underpins total dedication; the drive to make things happen and the 'in it together' mentality that unites.

This experience also reminds me what a great job I have! Being on 'the inside' working with people performing at the highest level and, consequently, in the public eye, brings with it an exhilaration and buzz that I have both thrived on and learned hugely from. It has also brought with it a responsibility to 'not mess up'. Helping leaders make decisions that affect whole organisations, and advising and guiding those who are putting everything on the line to get the best out of themselves, requires a composure and objectivity that is sometimes hard to maintain.

I have worked with, advised and observed leaders at very close quarters in numerous performance settings. As well as the interventions described above, I have also worked with Olympic and World Champions, professional golfers, leaders in the performing arts, medicine, charities and organisations across virtually the whole business sector spectrum. My experience is that the issues and challenges facing leaders are fundamentally the same whatever the setting.

A lot of this work has been on a one-to-one basis with leaders in high-profile positions, where the confidential and independent nature of my profession has meant that I have got to know them intimately as both professionals and as human beings. These are people who have the same frailties and vulnerabilities as those they lead; the problem for them is that they feel unable to own up to them for fear of losing credibility and following. Their existence can sometimes be a lonely one.

Learning on the job

So much of what I talk about and do with leaders is based on my own experience of being a leader. I cut my leadership teeth in the university world, where I created and grew a team of academic staff and doctoral students. It was here that I learned about leading and developing a close-knit unit capable of holding its own in an ego-driven and highly political environment. Looking back on that time, it was also here where I made the mistake of following the conventional leadership approach that I am now devoting an entire book to challenging. I led in the only way I knew. My leadership exuded passion and care for the team I had put together because that is what I believed leadership was all about. Tempered by an environment outside the team that I perceived to be 'hostile' and uncaring, this led to a style of leadership which inspired loyalty; unfortunately, that loyalty was probably misplaced. My overcaring and overprotective approach was, in retrospect, probably parental and stifling. Yes, I inspired loyalty but I did not create the conditions where my team could develop, learn from mistakes and take ownership. I fought their 'battles' for them and this created animosity with other leaders and their teams. I worked *against* the environment rather than *with* it, my leadership being founded on the way I was, what I believed in and what had driven my success to that point rather than what was required.

Essentially, I had followed a leadership path, trodden by so many, where the person I was drove the way I led. The ensuing environment of dependence and lack of ownership within my team, together with the tension my approach engendered outside the team, meant I will never know what we could actually have achieved. The team was successful in delivering against all assigned performance measures, but how good could we have *really* been? Leading in the way I knew best created a sub-optimal environment that in turn resulted in what almost certainly was under-achievement, or at least a failure to deliver our full potential. Put simply, following the 'leadership – environment – performance' path was the wrong approach!

I was able to apply the invaluable learning from that early experience when I left the academic world to co-found Lane4 Management Group Ltd, a company that employs the elite sporting metaphor as a source of learning in commercial organisations. It was here where I worked with leaders and their teams in organisations such as Deutsche Bank, British Airways, HSBC, Sainsbury's, DaimlerChrysler, Manchester Airport, Microsoft, Accenture, GE, Linklaters, the Post Office, J.P. Morgan, St Mary's Hospital in Paddington and too many others to list here.

This is when a lot of the advice I passed on to leaders was increasingly driven and founded not only by the scientific research I had 'grown up on' as an academic, but also by my own experiences and continuing development as a leader growing an organisation. And what an experience! Lane4 grew from nothing to an international business with more than seventy people and a turnover of more than £7m. It was not an entirely smooth ride, of course, and I experienced both the highs and lows of being a leader. Managing expectations, aspirations, conflict, politics, uncertainty, change, demanding clients, cash-flow worries and unpopular messages are all part of being a leader and I have been right at the core of the pressure that is unavoidable.

In 2010 I left Lane4 to embark on a new adventure in the form of establishing Top Performance Consulting Ltd, where I continue to love the work I do with leaders and their teams and being able to put my own 'on-the-job' training as a leader into practice. I have gained so much from my own leadership experiences, but my most important learning is about the need to focus on performance first, and being crystal clear about what 'performance' *actually* means. It is only when this has been clearly defined that leaders can identify with confidence what the performance environment should look and feel like. And only then, of course, can the leader conclude how to lead. Define performance, identify the environment needed to deliver it, and lead accordingly. 'Performance – environment – leadership'; simple!

Who is this book for?

The book is intended to appeal to, and provide an important resource for, a broad range of readers across the whole spectrum of domains, settings, sectors and contexts with performance at their core. It will be useful to current leaders aiming to enhance their leadership capability in preparation for stepping up to the next level, as well as others who find themselves in challenging situations and circumstances such as recovering from failures and setbacks, leading 'turnarounds', leading a merger or acquisition, overseeing a downsizing exercise, and simply being new to a leadership role.

The book will also be useful for leaders who wish to enhance their team leadership skills. Whether they range from high-performing teams to dysfunctional working groups, from close-knit to virtual, and from newly formed to long-standing, teams present a challenge for all leaders. Big egos, big brains, strong characters, personality clashes and entrenched mindsets are never far away in teams, and this book will help leaders with their approach to and management of them.

Aspiring leaders will also benefit from reading the book, especially those who are part of leadership and talent development programmes. These can be intensely ambitious people who want to reach the top rung of the leadership ladder as quickly as possible. They are out to impress and short-circuit the system if possible; if successful, these people reach leadership positions for which they may not yet be equipped, and there are harsh lessons ahead of them. Sometimes the people on these programmes are not always the 'willing volunteers' you might expect. They have been identified as having 'leadership potential' and find themselves on a programme that sets them on a path they would not necessarily have chosen. Not all leaders 'choose' to be leaders but end up in leadership positions anyway. Leadership can be a real challenge for these people too.

The book is also intended as a resource for people who are involved in partnering or supporting leaders in their personal development and also the development of their organisations and teams. Leadership and development, human resource and organisational development specialists, in particular, will find this an invaluable guide and support for their interventions and impact.

What is this book about?

The core focus of the book is on the whole experience of being a leader and everything that accompanies it. At its core is a very simple model of leadership applicable across all performance settings: define 'performance', then identify the 'environment' required to deliver it, and then 'lead' accordingly (this is referred to as the 'PEL Model' in the remainder of the book). It is not a book of *answers*, nor is it a *self-help guide* or a list of things *to do* as a leader. Instead, it is more a book on what is at the core of being a leader and how to think about and approach the responsibility of leadership and what it entails.

The whole essence of the book is founded on the responsibility of leaders to deliver performance of the highest quality which is sustainable; this is 'Top Performance Leadership'. Therefore, there is a big emphasis on 'performance' in the book to stimulate leaders to think about performance in ways they have probably not considered previously. The 'environment' leaders create also figures prominently and in a way that is designed to encourage them to leave no stone unturned in enabling sustainable top performance.

The content includes some ideas that have appeared in my earlier books on 'pressure' because that is an inextricable part of being a leader[3][4]. It also addresses the motives that drive leaders, again an inextricable part of being a leader, in the form of 'real' and 'safe' leadership[5]. However, the vast majority of the book is based upon new material. For example, the section on 'sustainable leadership' is based on a study I published recently[6], and the sections on 'team leadership', 'performance' and 'environment' are areas I have not written about in previous books.

Finally, the book is designed to be exhaustive of the demands on leaders and the 'things' they need to focus on and ensure are in place. There may at times appear to be a lot to think about as a top performance leader, and also a lot for you to absorb as a reader – and there is! But stick with it because this is the reality of top performance leadership. The leader must ensure nothing is left to chance in identifying, reflecting on and catering for every possibility, probability and certainty in their quest to deliver top performance that is sustainable.

Looking to others' experiences: the Advisory Board

The content of my previous books has been based on my own published research in peer-reviewed scientific literature. Whilst

---

3 G. Jones. *Thrive On Pressure: Lead And Succeed When Times Get Tough.* New York: McGraw-Hill, 2010.
4 G. Jones & A. Moorhouse. *Developing Mental Toughness: Gold Medal Strategies For Enhancing Your Business Performance.* Oxford: Spring Hill, 2008.
5 See 3 above.
6 G. Jones. 'The role of Superior Performance Intelligence in sustained success'. In S.Murphy (Ed), *The Oxford Handbook Of Sport And Performance Psychology.* Oxford: Oxford University Press, 2012.

large parts of the content of this book are based on my own and others' published research, the model forming the core of it is based on my experience of working with leaders. Since the model is positioned to challenge current leadership practices across organisations in all performance domains, I was keen to subject it to validation by people who collectively represent a broad range of experience and expertise.

I approached five people who agreed to act in an advisory capacity for the book and have given them the grand title of 'Advisory Board'. The collective experience and expertise of this team covers a broad range of performance domains; specifically, large business organisations, the Third Sector, medicine, sport and the military. Let me introduce them to you briefly.

- **Dr Jonathan Goldman MD** has medical experience as the leader of heart-disease teams in major hospitals in the UK and US, as well as experience of large business organisations as a senior leader in biotechnology and pharmaceutical companies
- **Graham Hodgkin** is the chief executive officer of a charity and also has vast experience of large business organisations as a former leader in corporate banking
- **John Peters** has extensive military experience as a fighter pilot and facilitator of programmes on leadership and performance in aviation, as well as consulting on leadership, strategy and change in a broad range of organisations
- **Dominic Sheldrick** is an ex-elite swimmer who competed for Australia in the 1980s and has worked closely with leaders in organisations spanning several sectors
- **Sue White** is a group HR director with extensive experience of strategic leadership, working internationally and business partnering with leaders in numerous large organisations

These people were asked to:

- Provide feedback on the entire working manuscript as it evolved, reinforcing or challenging aspects of the content where appropriate
- Provide an independent written commentary on the PEL Model which forms the core of the book and its applicability to the organisations and sectors they have worked in

The Advisory Board have played a crucial role in the process of testing and validating my challenge around conventional leadership practices. Their commentaries feature in the final part of the book in which they share examples and insights which reinforce and bring to life the PEL Model.

The detailed feedback they have provided on the manuscript has proved immensely valuable in reinforcing and also challenging the content, as well as provoking and further shaping my thinking. Consequently, the content that follows is based not just on my own experience and research but also, and more importantly, on the broad-ranging experiences and expertise of people who are highly qualified in the areas of leadership and performance.

Part 1

Top Performance Leadership
Where do you start?

1.1 Why would anyone want to be a leader?

The sheer volume of texts on being a leader has already been alluded to in the Introduction and is testimony to a challenge that requires fine balancing skills. On the one hand, as shown in Figure 1.1.1, being a leader can be inspiring, exhilarating and enjoyable; on the other hand, it can also be frustrating, stressful and overwhelming. Whether documented in the form of biographies, theories, models, metaphors, parables or wisdom, leadership attracts a broad and diverse audience hungry for tips, tricks, strategies and tools to give themselves the best chance of making the leadership experience a positive one.

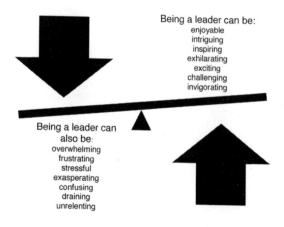

Figure 1.1.1 Leadership is a fine balancing act

Not long ago, in preparation for a keynote presentation on what makes a good leader, I randomly selected fifteen books from my hefty collection on leadership and conducted a 'not very scientific' content analysis of them. Essentially, I scanned through each one and listed all of the attributes, qualities and skills the various authors highlighted as important. Apparently, being a good leader requires you to be and do all of the things listed in Figure 1.1.2.

Be a good communicator
Have a clear vision
Be a meticulous planner
Make the right decisions
Be self-assured
Be a good people manager
Instill belief
Be inspiring
See the big picture
Be intellectually astute
Show passion
Be a mentor
Have a high tolerance for stress
Be a good listener
Know the relevant detail
Problem-solve
Remain calm in adversity
Be optimistic
Know your people's names
Be emotionally intelligent
Be a team player
Learn from mistakes
Care about your people
Be innovative
Coach
Be visible
Let people make mistakes
Balance the short- and long-term

Address underperformance
Command loyalty
Empower people
Handle conflict
Deliver the strategy
Recognise good performance
Delegate
Recruit good people
Be a good negotiator
Drive change
Tell it like it is
Be determined
Have integrity
Take risks
Trust people
Have charisma
Be a good influencer
Involve people in decisions
Show empathy
Be your own person
Seek feedback
Be able to give bad news
Set goals
Build team spirit
Know what drives people
Make people accountable
Set high expectations
Deliver the results

Figure 1.1.2 The demanding world of leadership.

This list is ample demonstration of just how hard it is to be a good leader. And that is based on only fifteen books! Imagine if this list included everything from *all* of the books on leadership! Oh, and by the way, whilst working hard to focus on and do all these things well, leaders are also reminded of the need to achieve a good work-life balance!

Living with the consequences of being a leader

It is not only the books that can make leadership seem overwhelming at times. My experiences of working with leaders in a variety of performance arenas leave me in no doubt that it can be a tough role. If the volume and diversity of 'things' leaders are supposed to be good at is not challenging enough, then the overriding accountabilities and responsibilities they must assume are undeniably daunting.

What are these accountabilities and responsibilities? At the most fundamental level, as shown in Figure 1.1.3, leadership begins with establishing a clear vision; people want to know *where* their leader intends to take them and *why*. And this desire permeates all levels of organisations. All too often, leaders who are not right at the top of the hierarchy assume visions are for the whole organisation only, failing to realise that it is 'local' visions – closely aligned with the organisation's vision – that engage and drive people's behaviours. So any leader of any team in any organisation who has not somehow identified a vision for the team is abdicating an important responsibility. I will return to this and why some leaders shy away from visions later in the book.

Next, leaders need to formulate a strategy and plan so that their people know *how* the vision will be achieved and what is expected of them. Clarity around roles and boundaries, who is tasked with what and ensuring deployment of appropriate skills and expertise where they can be maximised, are all crucial components the leader has to get right.

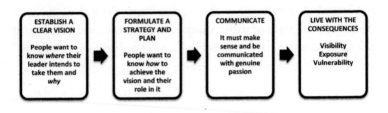

Figure 1.1.3 Living with the consequences of being a leader.[1]

The vision and strategy must then be communicated to the people who are being asked to deliver it. This is the point where leaders must exhibit a level of logic that is bulletproof if they are to secure their people's buy-in and engagement. In communicating the vision and strategy, leaders must also show genuine emotion, oozing a passion that will inspire everyone to follow. They can never be off their guard, and sometimes make the mistake of forgetting their people's eyes and ears are continually watching and listening for confirmation that they genuinely believe in the vision or sometimes, sadly, reinforcement that the boss is not really committed to it and is merely 'talking a good game'.

This is a potential pitfall for all leaders and the realisation that they are communicating with their people all the time is crucial to success. Chris Rodgers, in his book, *Informal Coalitions*[2], describes four separate aspects of leadership communication, shown in Figure 1.1.4, which draws out this point. The various forms are distinguished by the degree

1 From G. Jones. *Thrive On Pressure: Lead And Succeed When Times Get Tough*. New York: McGraw-Hill, 2010.
2 C. Rodgers. *Informal Coalitions: Mastering the Hidden Dynamics of Organisational Change*. Basingstoke: Palgrave Macmillan, 2007.

of *structure* where 'structured' communication is planned in advance and efforts are made to contain outcomes within management-controlled boundaries, whilst 'unstructured' communication is unplanned and spontaneous. The degree of *formality* that each of them involves is the other distinguishing factor. 'Formal' communication involves the passing of messages from leaders to staff, whilst 'informal' communication involves joint sense-making.

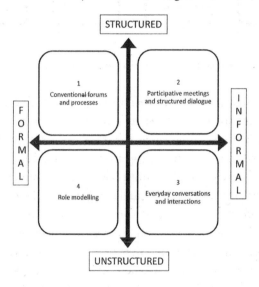

Figure 1.1.4 Leadership communication grid.[3]

Quadrants 1 and 2 in Figure 1.1.4 are the forms of communication that leaders are very conscious of and have the opportunity to prepare for. Structured and formal communication (1) includes established forums, processes and techniques in the form of media such as 'town hall' presentations, newsletters and the intranet. This is the conventional notion of leadership communication where the leader

---

3 Based on Rodgers (2007).

is in the spotlight and people are being given the information deemed necessary and appropriate by the leadership. Structured and informal communication (2) includes events such as participative meetings, focus groups and 'breakfast with the boss' sessions designed to produce joint decisions and problem solving.

Quadrants 3 and 4 represent what Rodgers refers to as the 'messy' forms of communication that leaders do not always recognise they are engaged in but are actually more impactful than the other two. Unstructured and informal communication (3) involves the everyday informal conversations that leaders have in corridors, at the coffee machine and the like. Unstructured and formal communication (4) highlights the impact of the behaviours or role modelling that others see in their leader. It is formal because of the one-way messaging that observers 'make of it what they wish'.

This whole process of establishing and then communicating and living a clear vision and strategy in ways they are not always aware of means that leaders will be highly visible, exposed and vulnerable. Many of the most senior leaders I have worked with are so visible and exposed that they sometimes feel isolated and lonely; these can be some of the unfortunate consequences leaders must live with if they are to do it well. Confusion may ensue when leaders find that everyone wants to be their friend. In fact, they have so many 'friends' that they are sometimes unable to identify who their true friends and allies really are.

Such visibility and exposure can weigh very heavily on the shoulders of leaders. The expectations of their people and of themselves can be enormous, to the extent where they may secretly wonder if they are up to it. I have been told by a number of leaders when we are behind closed doors, 'I'm waiting to be found out' or 'I'm wondering how I got to this position; I don't feel comfortable in it'. As I alluded to in the Introduction, some people who find themselves in leadership positions may not actually want to *be* leaders! In the legal profession, for example, I have come across people who have achieved senior partner status, that coveted 'badge' signifying their worth to the firm as a lawyer and valued colleague, who have struggled with the added expectation that this means they now have to step up to be leaders as well. They signed up to be lawyers, not leaders!

The responsibilities and accountabilities of leaders do not, of course, cease when they have secured the buy-in of people via a compelling vision communicated with passion. The demands are incessant as they become dominated by the daily grind of operating in an environment where they are expected to be decisive, know the answers, be role models and deliver the results. Get it wrong, and leaders can lose many of those newly acquired 'friends and allies'.

I witnessed these very circumstances at close quarters when I worked as psychologist to the Wales rugby union team. The man in charge at the time was Graham Henry, a New Zealander who had become the highest-paid rugby union coach in the world and was continually reminded of the expectations accompanying such a salary under the burning spotlight of a fanatical Welsh media and public. The early part of his tenure had brought the success they had longed for as he guided the team to eleven consecutive victories over countries which included the arch enemy, England, and a first-ever win against South Africa. Henry's team was successful and he was a hero. The media nicknamed him 'The Great Redeemer', but it was not to last. Things began to derail when his team lost to lesser opposition in poor performances and, before long, was in the middle of its worst run since he took charge.

The media who had built Henry up to be a great coach quickly became his biggest critic. He stopped reading the newspapers and watching the television sports news. He stopped going out in public because of the open, almost spitting abuse he received from fans who spotted him. I witnessed some of it and it was venomous and intolerable. When the team enjoyed success, Henry had been surrounded by people who wanted to share in it; now the failure was his alone to bear. The 'new' place he found himself in was a very lonely one; he was exposed and highly vulnerable. The enormous expectations and, at that time, the lack of depth of quality among the players required to deliver sustained success, eventually got the better of a great coach and a good man; he left the job by 'mutual agreement' with his bosses.

Stepping beyond functional expertise

People generally get promoted to leadership positions because they are good at what they do. But leadership is not about being a good accountant, lawyer, investment banker and the like. The mistake most organisations make is that they move people up through the organisation because of what they have achieved to date using their functional skills, experience and expertise. They then find themselves having to bring in people like myself to help these leaders understand how to lead their people.

There is no better example of this than in the world of academia, where people who may be great scientists, mathematicians, philosophers or engineers work their way up the hierarchical ladder by being just that. However, the further these academics clamber up the rungs, the further they find themselves removed from the comfort of their core competencies. Their prowess as academics is never in doubt. However, many do not have the people skills, know-how and/or inclination required to be effective and respected leaders. Inept leadership by very good academics is one of the reasons why I am no longer in the academic world.

Leadership is all about people, and people are hard to lead! They have opinions and views on how things should be done. Some of them may think they can do a better job at leading than their leader. They have feelings, moods and emotions, which are sometimes unpredictable, unexpected and inexplicable. People have different lives outside organisations which they may or may not want their bosses to know about. Their motivation, confidence and personalities all need to be considered and factored into any interactions. They have frailties and make mistakes; they like to be praised and to be made to feel good about themselves. Some of them want responsibility and accountability, whilst others prefer to be told what to do. Some of them are to be trusted, others are not; some are loyal to their leader, others are not. All of these ways in which people differ, and the many more too numerous to list here, mean that leading is hard. That is why many leaders focus on managing tasks and the operations – it is what they are good at, and it's a lot easier than leading people!

If all of the above does not constitute a demanding enough challenge, then leaders are certainly tested when times are tough. Good economic climates hide many flaws in organisations, and poor leadership and inept leaders often go unnoticed in those favourable times. Too often, as long as the results are delivered, few questions are asked about 'how' they are delivered. But things are very different when times are tough and things are not going to plan, or perhaps when an organisation is going through major change. This is when outstanding leadership is so crucial; of course, it also just happens to be when outstanding leadership is so very difficult to deliver! Uncertainty and perceived lack of control mean that people need and want to be able to trust their leaders in these difficult times, so that being open and letting their staff know how things stand is paramount. People want their leaders to help them through the inevitable catastrophising, scaremongering and doom and gloom that can proliferate during change and turbulent times. Listening to their concerns, showing empathy and reminding them of the successes, however small, should always be at the forefront of the leader's mind in these circumstances. But leaders must also continue to focus on a strategy for moving forward and keeping their people focused on delivering quality services and products.

All this is demanded of leaders when they may be feeling pretty worried and pessimistic themselves! So in tough times, even the best leaders are stretched to their limits. What has worked in the past may not work so well in these difficult times.

So why *would* anyone want to be a leader?

I have, of course, deliberately painted the dark side of leadership to emphasise just how demanding it is to do well. When it is done right, it is very enjoyable and satisfying. Some of the reasons that excite many of the leaders I have worked with about their role include:

- The challenge that accompanies their visibility and accountability
- Getting people bought into and working towards common goals
- Having the opportunity to make things happen and make a difference
- Gaining the respect and loyalty of their people
- Helping people achieve what they thought was impossible
- Selecting and working with good people around them
- The buzz they get from delivering the results
- Seeing people grow and develop as a result of their coaching, mentoring and sometimes teaching

And there are numerous high-profile stories of successful leaders who have really struggled in the role to begin with, or who at various points in their tenure have come through inauspicious circumstances to turn things around to achieve things others may have doubted they could deliver. For example, I was delighted for Graham Henry when he guided the New Zealand All Blacks to their World Cup win in 2012. Microsoft's Bill Gates is another leader whose career turned out pretty well after his first business, Traf-O-Data, failed. And what of Abraham Lincoln, who went to war as a captain and returned a private (the lowest rank)? Even that 'great leader', Winston Churchill, did not achieve success in leadership roles until he became British Prime Minister at sixty-two years of age.

1.2 Top performance leadership

Facing what might seem like overwhelming demands and expectations, it is not surprising that many leaders choose the 'easy' option of taking a top-down approach to their roles. It is also the obvious option! Organisational structures are almost always drawn with leaders at the top, and leaders are expected to inspire followership among 'the people below'. All too often, the innocent use of that dreadful word 'subordinates' has the effect of further perpetuating the unchallenged notion of leaders being on top directing their minions, who follow their every command and cater to their every whim. And when leaders talk about 'cascading' their vision within the organisation, there is only one direction anything will ever cascade!

So the language, ethos and culture in the vast majority of organisations perpetuates and exacerbates what has become an unchallenged protocol that leaders should adopt a top-down approach to leadership. But what if leaders turned their profession on its head?

Turning leadership on its head

There are numerous theories and models of leadership, most overcomplicating a role that in actuality is quite straightforward. At the simplest level, leaders must deliver performance that will satisfy key stakeholders. If this performance is to be delivered and sustained, then leaders must oversee the creation of an environment which enables it to be delivered. In essence, therefore, there are three core elements to 'get right' in any organisation: the leadership, the environment and the performance.

But where do leaders start? This is where too many of them take the conventional route shown in Figure 1.2.1 and start with their own leadership – and why not? As we know, leaders almost always get promoted to leadership positions because of their personal attributes, whether experience, achievements, knowledge and/or skills – in other words, what they are good at. They have reached leadership positions because of who and what they are, so it is natural that they should start from and rely on what has got them to where they are.

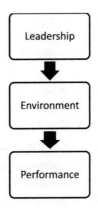

Figure 1.2.1 The conventional approach to leadership.

The environment these leaders create will inevitably reflect the stamp that they may sometimes subconsciously impose upon it. For example, leaders with a command-and-control approach in circumstances where it is inappropriate should not be surprised that the environment they oversee is dominated by fear and risk-aversion as their people avoid responsibility and accountability and await their next order. At the extreme, there is the danger of producing or promoting clones and delivering performance that is a direct function of the strengths of the leader, but also limited by his or her weaknesses. Leaders who are surrounded by like-minded people with similar skills and experiences may well deliver the performance that satisfies key stakeholders, but will this reflect the true potential of the people and the organisation? I have witnessed too many organisations whose performance has been constrained by the limitations of the senior leaders. Sadly, this is sometimes not just about capability but also about their motives: self-interest gets the better of them and the organisation comes second.

Putting top performance first

Top performance leadership is about putting performance first (see Figure 1.2.2). But it is more than *just* achieving the performance that will keep stakeholders happy; it is about the future health of the organisation. Leaders often focus too much on delivering numbers-driven, short-term Key Performance Indicators (KPIs) and targets that could jeopardise the organisation's future growth and sustainability. The top performance leadership approach involves thinking about performance in a way most leaders are unlikely to have previously contemplated. Performance is more than just an outcome or output; it is a process or paradigm involving meticulous planning and preparation, which culminates in a clearly defined and delivered end point. It involves being crystal clear in distinguishing between 'output', 'outcome' and 'impact', optimising the balance between effectiveness and efficiency, and developing the ability to regulate performance in rapid response to changing conditions and demands. Crucial to the process of delivering top performance is the ability to pinpoint the critical performance drivers and keep them in relentless focus.

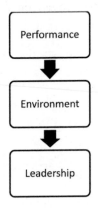

Figure 1.2.2 Top performance leadership: Where do you start?

Defining and creating the top performance environment

Top performance leadership then involves defining the internal environment that will deliver the performance. A key part of top performance leadership is selecting people who have the ability required to deliver top performance. But having great people does not guarantee success; even the very best performers will eventually struggle to deliver their best in an environment that is not conducive to their needs. The performance environment includes numerous factors to consider. What are the enablers and incentives that need to be in place to ensure the performance? What are the values that will drive success? What are the abilities, mindsets and behaviours required of those who will deliver the performance? Whatever the answers to these questions, my experience of working in numerous organisations across different performance domains informs me that there are critical factors that need to be satisfied in any organisation intent on delivering sustainable top performance:

- Leaders have worked hard to get the 'right people' in the 'right places' so that they are doing what they are *good at* and also what they *want* to do
- Individuals and teams are clear about what is expected of them on a day-to-day basis as well as in the longer-term
- People thrive in conditions created by the combination of top performance expectations that are accompanied by high levels of support to achieve them
- Delegation and empowerment are the norm, being underpinned by good working relationships, a feedback culture, accountability and ownership, and clearly defined goals
- There is a 'we're in it together' mentality that is the foundation of top-performing teams
- 'Healthy competition' exists in the form of shared learning and commitment to everyone's development, as well as individual and team goals being completely aligned
- Success is recognised and celebrated

It is only when the targeted performance has been identified, and then the environment required to deliver it has been defined, that top performance leadership can be mapped out.

Being a top performance leader

Top performance leadership is not about skills and abilities as such, but much more about:

- The *motives* that lie at the core of leaders and which drive their focus, behaviour and intent
- The *support* they are able to attract and harness from those closest to them
- The *know-how* they bring or develop as a leader, on which they are able to draw to sustain themselves

Top performance leaders' *motives* mean they are driven by a 'real' desire to make things happen rather than sitting back and playing it 'safe'. These leaders know that top-performing organisations are continually changing – they can never stand still. Whether it is driving internal change aimed at sustaining and enhancing people's engagement and the environment required to deliver the performance, or the continual innovation necessary to maintain and gain competitive advantage, top performance leaders strive to stay ahead of the game. This requires courage to challenge convention and to make and communicate decisions that they know will be unpopular but are in the best interests of the organisation. The tough issues that are the bane of many organisations are tackled quickly and head-on; hard conversations about things like underperformance and unproductive behaviours are never postponed.

Top performance leaders recognise that they cannot do all of this on their own, at least not in the longer-term, and that gaining the *support* of those closest to them is critical to the achievement of their aspirations for the organisation. They work hard to get the best fit-for-purpose people around them and take a close interest in their further professional and personal development. After all, it is in the leader's personal interests to ensure that the team is continually growing and that his or her coaching, mentoring and, sometimes, teaching skills are put to good use.

Unfortunately, this is not always the case. I have witnessed senior leaders so focused on what is going on 'out there' that they forget what is going on 'under their nose'. These leaders often oversee top-performing teams and people 'out there' in the organisation but find themselves as part of their own underperforming or even dysfunctional leadership team because members do not see themselves as a team. Rather, this is the forum where individuals come together to represent the parts of the organisation they are responsible for and the classic silo mentality prevails. They forget their role as a senior leadership team is to collaborate across functions and strong personalities, opinions, egos and self-interest can get the better of the need to be united. This is where top performance leaders really have their work cut out because they must work hard to ensure their own team is aligned, cohesive, supportive and driven by the best interests of the organisation. Team leadership is what top performance leaders are especially good at.

Finally, top performance leaders possess a *know-how* that enables them to get the best out of themselves and the broader external environment which they are able to draw on to sustain themselves, thus ensuring their leadership longevity. It allows them to stay in tune with their environment; they take nothing for granted, especially when it comes to their people's commitment, loyalty and engagement. They know that no matter how good a job they do as a leader, there will always be some people who are disgruntled and disengaged. They devote time and energy to listening to their people's views, showing genuine empathy and then acting accordingly.

The *know-how* possessed by top performance leaders also equips them in building and maintaining day-to-day relationships with colleagues at all levels. Like all of us, they may gravitate towards certain types of people, but they work hard to establish good relations with others they do not always connect with. They display humility where people come forward with ideas and feel comfortable telling them what they think. This ensures they keep abreast of what is happening in the environment so that they can deal with issues quickly.

Underpinning their sustainability as top performance leaders is the ability and *know-how* to lead themselves. In fact, it is unreasonable of anyone to expect to be a good leader of other people until they have learned to lead themselves. Top performance leadership involves being stretched because much of their time is spent operating outside their comfort zone. Adaptability, perseverance and self-belief are just some of the personal resources that will be called upon when times get especially tough and inevitable setbacks test these leaders' inner strength. And it is not only the lows that leaders must deal with; there will be plenty of highs and achievements to feel good about, and leading themselves effectively is as much about not getting carried away with success as it is about riding the lows.

1.3 Summary

There is nothing complex about top performance leadership; in fact, it is quite straightforward, if leaders start in the right place! This whole book is based on the simple PEL Model shown in Figure 1.3.1, which includes three core components – performance, environment and leadership – which, if leaders address in the 'right' order and get them 'right', will ensure the current and future health of any organisation.

In any sector, all organisations exist to deliver performance; this is the starting point. Top performance leaders oversee the detailed process of defining the *what*, *why*, *who*, *when* and *how* of top performance. They then focus on the environment, identifying and creating the conditions in which people can thrive and deliver top performance. Top performance leaders then lead accordingly to ensure the delivery of top performance that is sustainable.

PERFORMANCE
Define the What? Why? Who? When? How?

ENVIRONMENT
Create the conditions in which people can thrive

LEADERSHIP
Ensure the delivery of sustainable top performance

Figure 1.3.1 Top performance leadership: The PEL Model.

Part 2

Putting Top Performance First

Defining the What?, Why?, Who?, When? and How?

2.1 The 3D Model of Top Performance

There are many ways of thinking about performance but it is seldom viewed beyond the form of some clear outcome or output. Nowhere are outcomes and outputs more highly visible than in sport, where medals achieved, championships won and records broken are the source of endless discussion, speculation and envy. In the commercial world, the indicators driving organisations and their stakeholders are the turnover, profit/loss and share-price statistics that so publicly indicate success or failure. Numbers and targets are equally important in charities, medicine and the military, where they are likely to be more in a human capital form in terms of lives saved or lost. Deeper scrutiny of all performance arenas will reveal a multitude of other measures underpinning these headline statistics but, for now, the common denominator across the various performance domains is that you can assign a number to their respective outcomes and outputs.

However, there is much more to performance than merely delivering numbers and hitting targets. Systems, procedures, knowledge, plans, analysis, rehearsal, expertise, reviews, simulation, ability, experience, risk, standards, policies, skills and execution are just some of the variables that can be factored into the 'performance equation'. As with the concept of leadership, it can be difficult to know where to begin when confronted with the challenge of managing performance at this level of complexity. The best starting point is to view performance not only as an outcome or output but, more importantly, as the result of a process or paradigm which involves a meticulous focus on and implementation of three essential elements in the '3D Model of Top Performance' shown in Figure 2.1.1.

Defining top performance involves establishing the 'what, why and when?' *What* constitutes top performance, *why* and *when* it will be achieved will vary as a function of different conditions and circumstances; performance aspirations during a recession or rebuilding period, for example, will probably be different to what are expected during good times or when things are at a peak. Of paramount importance is that the *what, why* and *when* dimensions of performance expectations should always be clear to everyone involved.

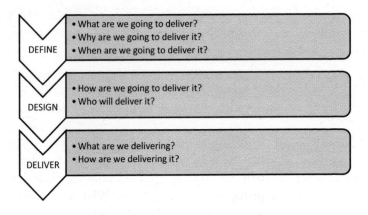

Figure 2.1.1 The 3D Model of Top Performance.

Designing top performance involves identifying and being specific about the 'how and who'. Performance is multifaceted and multidimensional, and the success of organisations in all performance sectors relies on identifying, clarifying and ensuring *how* the specific facets and dimensions are completely aligned and coordinated. *Who* has accountability and responsibility for ensuring that the various facets of the plan are carried out successfully must also be identified.

Delivering top performance is about regulating the 'what and how?' – performance levels need to be regulated to deliver top performance when required. Avoiding that one-off top performance which is not sustainable requires ensuring effectiveness *and* efficiency, as well as the careful monitoring and analysis of *what* is being delivered and *how* it is being delivered. This enables continual calibration and re-alignment where necessary, in addition to informing and shaping future performance aspirations.

The 3D Model of Top Performance is simple and common sense. However, common sense is not always common practice! Miss out or misalign any of the 3Ds and the likelihood of underachievement and/or failure increases to uncomfortable levels.

2.2 Defining top performance

Every time I pause during a presentation to ask the audience 'What is performance in your organisation?', I know it will be followed by a long list of measures, usually financially oriented, that will reel quickly and effortlessly off their tongues. Occasionally, someone recites the vision or perhaps a mission statement. What is *clear* is that in many organisations people are *unclear* as to what performance actually is beyond a series of looming deadlines and targets that must be met. Failure to establish and communicate the required clarity can lead to a hive of activity in which people work hard and long hours without really ever knowing what it is they are trying to achieve and therefore what to focus on. It also means that they can be denied the feeling of satisfaction of knowing they are doing a good job.

Recently I worked with one leadership team of a business that has enjoyed success over a sustained period, achieving year-on-year growth and profitability in a particularly difficult market sector. However, they recognised a 'more of the same' strategy would soon reach saturation and that they needed to do something different to help them and their business step up to the next level. What I found was a team of tired high achievers all working at a never-ending furious pace to achieve the company's vision of being 'excellent'. Our discussion of what 'excellent' actually looked and felt like unearthed different interpretations and assumptions that had never previously been raised, let alone debated. There was no defined end point, or even milestones, to their aspirations and it became abundantly clear that an unequivocal definition of *what* constituted 'excellent', *why* and by *when* was needed before entering into any discussion about how to step up to the next level.

Performance can be defined in numerous different ways, of course, so that discussions like this around establishing what performance actually is and will be in organisations requires some parameters and boundaries. This section identifies and describes a few important factors to consider which I have found to be particularly helpful in providing a framework for leaders to define performance for the organisation, team and themselves: 'creating visions that work', 'distinguishing between outputs, outcomes and impacts' and 'measuring performance'.

Creating visions that work

Visions seem to polarise opinion; people either love them or hate them. At best, visions can be powerful and impactful; they predict employee commitment[4] and ultimately organisational performance[5]. At worst, visions are not worth the paper, walls or slides they are

4   T. Dvir, N. Kass & B. Shamir. 'The emotional bond: Vision and organisational commitment among high-tech employees'. *Journal of Organisational Change Management,* 2004, 126–143.
5   R. Baum, E. Locke & S. Kirkpatrick. 'A longitudinal study of the relation of vision and vision communication to venture growth in entrepreneurial firms'. *Journal of Applied Psychology,* 1998, 43–54.

written on; few employees, if any, can recite the vision with accuracy, without hesitation and with enough passion and belief to inspire others to be sufficiently motivated to work towards it.

Creating a vision that inspires everyone to deliver extraordinary performance is difficult, which is why, as I described in Part 1.1, some leaders shy away. Other leaders and teams underestimate the challenge and plough on to create something that is flawed. Here are just a few of the ways in which leaders get it wrong when defining a vision:

- It has been created by the leadership behind closed doors
- It is not aligned with the organisation's shorter-term goals and aspirations
- It is couched so far into the future that people feel it has little relevance to their day-to-day work
- It is unveiled at a launch event in a transactional way and as a series of clinical statements about conquering the market sector, therefore lacking the emotional connection that will drive the desired behaviour
- The actions of the leaders are incongruent with the vision they themselves espouse
- The vision is merely a grand statement without a clear pathway to achieving it and can actually have a demotivating effect

Get it right and, as the evidence cited above endorses, a vision can have a powerful positive impact that could transform performance. If performance is to be defined in the form of a vision, then Dr Tara Jones's[6] ten 'rules' for creating, sharing and living visions urges leaders to:

1. Create a vision that *they* believe in and which excites *them*

---

6 T. Jones. 'What's your vision?' *Leadership Excellence*, March, 2010, 6–7

2. Consult as many people as possible from different parts of the organisation
3. Learn what motivates their people and also what frustrates and excites them
4. Ensure there is a clear alignment to key performance measures and performance management processes
5. Ensure the vision is clear and simple
6. Communicate the vision in a compelling way and with a clear time frame
7. Tell stories to bring the vision alive
8. Give their people the chance to make sense of the vision and what it means
9. Live the vision and show passion
10. Align their behaviours with the vision

These rules for creating, sharing and living the vision emphasise that having a vision is much more than a tick-box exercise. If followed carefully, they also mean that the resulting vision will be 'personal' to the organisation or team that has created it. This very factor means that it is difficult to highlight specific examples of 'good' visions. However, the best visions I have come across have been simply represented either in the form of a story or an image; visions do not have to be in the form of words or statements. Telling a story of the desired future and what it will be and feel like for the people in the organisation can be very powerful. A well-crafted vision story brings it alive and engenders personal meaning for all listeners.

A vision portrayed as an image can have a striking and immediate impact on people because it should need no explanation. Not long ago, I worked with a senior business development team in a large financial services organisation whose leader wanted to create a more cohesive team via a vision to which everyone contributed. Having failed to find the words to adequately capture their collective view of the future, the team eventually agreed on an image of the number-one Formula One racing team during a pit stop in a Grand Prix race. The image represented the metaphor for what they wanted to create for themselves and the teams reporting into them over the next eighteen months.

It showed the racing driver sitting in the car as the team worked furiously to change the tyres as quickly as possible; the driver represented the sales executives in the department who were at the centre of attention and highly rewarded for being successful. Of course, the driver's success was only possible with the support and hard work of the pit crew changing the wheels: these represented the staff in various support functions without whose dedicated effort the wheels would literally fall off. The person in the image with apparently the most straightforward job and who was largely unnoticed was the one standing at the front of the car holding the equivalent of a 'stop' and 'go' lollipop sign. However, if the 'lollipop man' turned the sign from 'stop' to 'go' a fraction too early, then the driver's success and well-being would be in serious danger; this character obviously represented the people in the support functions who appeared to have relatively menial jobs. The vision represented in this way was essentially of a team delivering success with the valued input of all involved; everyone had a significant part to play and all had to work together towards the same goal, whatever their level and function. This may appear obvious and simple to you and me but it had the effect of making everybody in the team fully aware of the importance and value of their roles in achieving the vision, and enabled them to be fully engaged with it.

As the ten rules described above emphasise, identifying a compelling vision in whatever form is worthless unless accompanied by regular reinforcement and the aligned day-to-day focus and role modelling of leaders. The Formula One image was made highly visible on the walls of the department and was referred to regularly in formal meetings, as well as becoming part of the department's language in informal interactions and conversations.

Finally, the rules also represent another example of common sense that is not always common practice: leaders know all this 'stuff' really but often fail to carry out the obvious because they are distracted by their own busyness. Following the essence of the ten rules will give them the best chance of defining a vision which will drive the attitudes, mindsets and behaviours to deliver within their prescribed time frame.

Distinguishing between outputs, outcomes and impacts

The distinctions between 'outputs', 'outcomes' and 'impacts' and their implications for focus, effort and ultimate performance can be subtle yet important in the context of defining performance. In their simplest forms:

- An 'output' is the product of an activity
- An 'outcome' is the result or consequence of the output
- An 'impact' is the meaning or significance of the outcome

Figure 2.2.1 draws out the fundamental differences using some clear examples from the worlds of business, the Third Sector and sport.

Dyson Limited is an organisation known initially for its innovation in the vacuum-cleaner market. The story behind the invention and production of the bagless vacuum is well-known and reflects a tale of personal tenacity, resilience and belief on the part of the founder, James Dyson. But it is also a story that provides a clear example of the distinction between outputs, outcomes and impacts. The use of dual cyclone technology to produce the *output* of the first bagless vacuum cleaner had the *outcome* of making it the biggest-selling product of its type in the UK within eighteen months and Dyson becoming the market leader. The *impact* was to revolutionise the vacuum-cleaner market and at the same time create the foundation for Dyson's further innovation and subsequent penetration of broader product markets.

	Output	Outcome	Impact
Dyson Ltd	Bagless vacuum	Market leader	Revolutionised the vacuum-cleaner market
Cancer Research UK	Financial donations	Fund cancer research	Improved cancer prevention, diagnosis and treatment
Dick Fosbury	'Fosbury Flop'	1968 Olympic Gold Medal	Revolutionised the high jump

Figure 2.2.1 Outputs, outcomes and impacts: Some examples.

The second example in Figure 2.2.1 is that of a Third Sector organisation, Cancer Research UK. Organisations such as this have a particular interest, of course, in their performance impact; indeed, it is what underpins their very existence, with the outputs and outcomes being an important means to an end. Clearly evident as one of Cancer Research UK's key *output* measures is the number and value of financial donations. Donations have the *outcome* of funding cancer research with the intended *impact* being the improvement in the prevention of cancer as well as diagnosis, treatment and care for people with the disease.

The final example, that of high jumper Dick Fosbury, further draws out the distinction between outputs, outcomes and impacts but also provides a contrasting approach to the previous example. Charities almost exclusively set out to identify their intended impact and then work on how to achieve it through outputs and outcomes. Fosbury's approach was to focus on the output and to perfect jumping over a high jump backwards, with the outcome being his gold medal success at the 1968 Olympics. He probably never dreamed of the impact it would have on his sport. Four years later, in Munich, twenty-eight of the forty competitors used Fosbury's technique. By 1980, thirteen of the sixteen Olympic finalists used it. Nearly fifty years later, it is the most popular technique in modern high jumping.

Defining performance in terms of outputs and outcomes is not new, of course, but considering the impact is not commonly factored into discussions around performance. Outputs and outcomes on their own can lead to a transactional relationship between an organisation's leaders and its employees. In the business sector, for example, employees may view their contribution to delivering them as merely lining the pockets of shareholders. Building in and ensuring a continual emphasis on the impact, or 'why?', dimension can be transformational in providing people with a greater sense of meaning and purpose, therefore enhancing engagement and commitment.

The benefits of distinguishing between outputs, outcomes and impacts apply equally well at organisational, team and individual levels. Identifying and focusing on the impact leaders and their teams would like to make, on whom and when, can help them through times when they are struggling with their motivation and need a reminder of why they should get out of bed in the morning.

Measuring performance: KPIs and CPIs

The process of defining performance inevitably involves defining how it will be measured. Performance measures in organisations, most commonly referred to as Key Performance Indicators (KPIs), do much more than provide a means of tracking performance; they are highly visible representations of what matters and is rewarded in organisations. They drive the culture and all the things that are subsumed under that: attitudes, behaviours, expectations, focus, decision-making etc. Consequently, measuring performance brings with it a raft of potential pitfalls and dilemmas. Get it wrong and the implications can be unfortunate and even disastrous.

A classic case in point is where business unit and team leaders are tasked with fostering a culture of collaboration in the form of sharing responsibility and accountability in an environment where performance is driven and rewarded through individualised targets and bonuses which are not always aligned. It is extremely difficult to turn a culture underpinned by self-focus and unhealthy competition into one of collaboration without a fundamental shift in the approach to KPIs. However, going too far in the opposite direction by having only collective KPIs can also cause problems. People watch one another closely to monitor if their contributions and efforts are worthy of the same rewards as themselves. Resentment, backstabbing and blame are some of the less attractive consequences of getting KPIs wrong.

The process of identifying KPIs also carries the danger of arriving at an unmanageable amount; many organisations have too many KPIs, which are also sometimes at odds with one another. I was recently asked to consult with a senior leader in a sales organisation who had been appointed to the newly created 'performance director' role. His remit was to make sense of, and draw together in one unifying framework, 175 KPIs that existed in different parts of the company. Unsurprisingly, he did not know where to start. This is where Richard Koch's '80/20 principle'[7] can be helpful. This principle is based on 80 per cent of results flowing from 20 per cent

---

7 R. Koch. *'The 80/20 principle: The secret of achieving more with less'.* London: Nicholas Brealey, 2004.

of causes. If the performance director had applied this principle, then he would have known to start by identifying the thirty-five indicators that cause the remaining 140.

Even thirty-five KPIs can seem a daunting and unmanageable prospect. I have learned from experiences like this that KPIs can actually dilute people's focus and distract them from what really matters. This is where the 80/20 principle needs some refinement to fit this specific context, and to what I propose should be more like a 95/5 ratio. In other words, for every 100 KPIs there are probably five that drive the rest; I have called these 'Critical' Performance Indicators (CPIs).

A classic metaphor for the KPI/CPI distinction can be found in the cockpit of modern aircraft. It is not so long ago that the average aeroplane had more than 100 cockpit instruments and controls competing for space and, more importantly, for pilot attention. This was a challenge for any pilot to absorb, process and act on, and concerted efforts to simplify aircraft operation have resulted in the identification of what are known as the 'Big Five' instruments that are critical to keeping all aeroplanes in the air: airspeed indicator, altimeter, artificial horizon, heading indicator and vertical speed indicator. These are the CPIs that, in the earlier cockpit design, were 'lost' among a vast array of information that was potentially overwhelming and distracting. This is the very essence of the distinction between KPIs and CPIs.

I remember from my early days as one of the leaders of a rapidly growing company how our focus was on developing a plethora of measures of customer satisfaction and new business development that we would track relentlessly. It took some time and experience to realise that these were only important so long as we had a healthy cash flow – no cash flow, no business! Looking back, the customer satisfaction and new business development measures were the KPIs, but the CPI that meant our business had a future was the minimisation of debtor days.

CPIs are what make the real difference in achieving top performance. They should be relatively few in number and defined simply and clearly to avoid any confusion. Of course, they should be in total alignment with each other and with the future aspirations and current needs of the organisation. Identifying specific CPIs can be difficult since they are not always the indicators staring leaders in the face, and they may not be easy to measure. This is where learning from performance domains such as the performing arts and sport can be so invaluable. For example, it is clear how important belief and focus are in enabling ballet dancers, musicians and athletes to achieve great things. Many of them 'target' belief and focus, and work towards achieving a level and sustainability that becomes one of their core goals.

Attributes such as focus and belief are difficult to measure, of course, which means there is a risk that this type of indicator might be neglected. A common example of a CPI often neglected or perhaps taken for granted in organisations is internal communication. My experience tells me that poor internal communication is a major source of underachievement and can be the reason why KPIs are not hit. The ensuing focus on improving KPIs achieves nothing more than plastering over the cracks whilst the cause is left unaddressed because it has not been identified as critical. Only after the identification of internal communication as a CPI will an intense focus and effort be devoted to it. Get it right and its impact on performance across all KPIs could be amazing.

In defining performance, therefore, it is important for leaders to identify the performance indicators that are critical for the success of their organisation, team and themselves. If they are not already measured, then ways of measuring them, or at the very least identifying processes for maintaining an intense focus on them, must be found.

2.3 Designing top performance

Would you set out on a journey to a new destination without having worked out exactly how to get there? Some organisations and teams do just that! They spend a lot of time defining and being very clear about the *what*, *why* and *when* but then make the mistake of not devoting sufficient, or sometimes any, time to working out the *how* and *who*.

Of course, there are numerous ways of designing performance and there is insufficient space here to cover them all. However, there is much to be learned from the sport, medical and military arenas, where attention to detail is meticulous and nothing is left to chance. This section describes two approaches that I have found particularly impactful in helping organisations, teams and individuals design how they will deliver their aspirations; 'setting outcome, output and input goals' and 'managing performance tensions'.

Setting outcome, output and input goals

The intense focus on the achievement of targets in short time frames prevalent in so many organisations can distract their people from devoting sufficient attention to the important processes underpinning performance. Indeed, countless people have informed me of the extremely challenging targets they have been set, but with relatively little guidance and support on *how* to achieve them.

The situation is different in other performance domains. In sport, there tends to be a much greater emphasis and focus on the processes underlying performance. Sport performers' time is very structured in the form of physical training and skills and strategy practice so that key processes are well defined and rehearsed. In medicine, getting the processes right is critical when 'disruptive' new products, devices or operations become available which change the standard of care. New skills and awareness must be absorbed very quickly since lives are at stake. The same is the case in the military, of course, where getting the process wrong can also have serious consequences. I witnessed this at first-hand when working alongside Royal Marine trainers whose job was quite literally to drill core skills and practices into young recruits. The focus was very much on getting the processes right time and again, with no tolerance of error. This rigorous attention to planning and preparation is where leaders in organisations in other performance arenas can learn a lot.

One particular means of designing performance that has been used for many years in elite sport and which has proved to have a strong impact when applied in other performance settings is based on the principle that performance goals can be broken down into three types of sub-goal: outcome, output and input goals. 'Outcomes' were defined earlier as the consequences of outputs, with 'outputs' defined as the products of activities. The additional dimension introduced here, 'input', is simply the means by which outputs are delivered. Designing performance using this framework involves identifying goals for each and ensuring all three types of goal are connected and totally aligned, as depicted in Figure 2.3.1. When operationalised in this way, outcome goals are the 'desired' high-level aspirations that 'require' achievement of output goals to realise them. Output goals, in turn, rely on the successful implementation of 'process' input goals underpinning them.

Since this approach has its heritage in elite sport, I will use a sport metaphor to clarify the difference between outcome, output and input goals. If you ask a world-top-ten golfer his goal for the tournament he is playing in next week, then he is likely to tell you that he 'wants to win'. This is quite natural, of course, but the problem is that there will be over 100 golfers starting the tournament, all with the same goal but with only one of them able to achieve it. If the golfer in question fails to win, then he has failed to achieve his goal. Golfers playing at this level therefore have more than one goal. The goal 'to win' is a *desired outcome* goal, as shown in Figure 2.3.2, but the outcome is not within the golfer's control. He could play brilliantly, but come second to another golfer who has performed even more outstandingly.

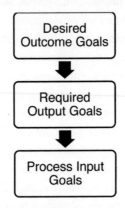

Figure 2.3.1 Outcome, output and input goals.

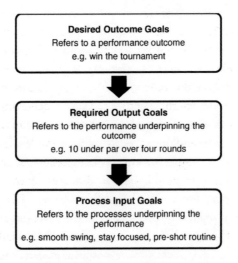

Figure 2.3.2 Designing top performance in golf.

The golfer in question will, therefore, set two other types of goal, both of which are under his total control. The example of a *required output* goal the golfer might set is his own score after the four rounds that comprise his performance in the tournament. In this example, he has figured out that, given the course conditions and weather forecast, ten under par should be good enough to win this particular tournament, something completely under his control. Underpinning the golfer's output goal are *process input* goals. The examples of 'smooth swing', 'staying focused' and a well-rehearsed 'pre-shot routine' are again completely under his control and underpin the achievement of his output goal.

An important factor in designing performance in this way is to ensure that the three different types of goal are planned and totally aligned towards the same ends. I used a sports example above to highlight how the different types of goal fit together, but the process is also a powerful tool for use in the business world. The example below is based on work I was involved in with the leadership team of a pharmaceutical company. They defined their desired outcome as a steady upward performance curve over the next two years that would ensure they had the highest share of the market within that time. Figure 2.3.3 shows the output goals required to deliver this outcome, as well as the core process input goals that would form the day-to-day focus in achieving the output.

As well as demonstrating the importance of carefully aligning outcome, output and input goals, this example also draws out another significant aspect of designing performance in this way; it centres around *who* should set the different levels of goal. The leadership team were clearly responsible for identifying the desired outcome, the 'what', but then involved the business unit and team leaders, who assumed the mantle of being the main drivers in identifying the specific detail regarding the required outputs in the form of growth in product and sales. The process input goals called for the input of team leaders and their people at the coalface, who agreed with the business units' heads about how the outputs would be achieved. Their input was paramount since they were the people tasked with achieving them.

Figure 2.3.3 Designing top performance in a pharmaceutical organisation.

Starting with the end in mind is fundamental to the process of designing performance in this way. This top-down approach involves identifying the desired outcome, required outputs and then the key process inputs that will enable them to be achieved. However, putting the plan into action on a day-to-day basis requires a bottom-up approach, with the major focus being on process inputs. The continual focus on getting the processes right will eventually deliver the outputs and, in turn, the outcomes.

Managing performance tensions

Getting the strategic focus right is vital in delivering top performance that is sustainable. Where leaders direct their focus is critical because it is a limited resource – they only have so much of it – so there is no margin for it to be even slightly misaligned with the defined performance aspirations. The defined performance will, of course, determine the specific areas of focus required, but discerning them among the vast number and array of potential distractors competing for leaders' attention can prove surprisingly formidable and sometimes perplexing. This is where the Managing Performance Tensions framework described in this section is particularly helpful in providing a simple and practical tool that leaders can use to guide them through the process of getting the strategic focus right.

The framework is grounded in research which indicates that performance involves the management of two dynamic tensions[8], each representing factors in the environment that compete for leaders' attention:

- **'Current' versus 'future'.** A 'current' focus involves attending to the short-term performance, efficiency and stability of the organisation. A 'future' focus involves attending to longer-term stability, flexibility and change initiatives. Strong focus on the 'current' means there is little focus left for the 'future', and vice versa.
- **'Internal' versus 'external'.** An 'internal' focus is largely on organisational capability through its people, systems and processes. An 'external' focus is directed towards stakeholder demands, a competitive position and differentiation in the marketplace. A strong 'internal' focus means little focus is left for the 'external' end of the continuum, and vice versa.

---

8 Based on R. Quinn & J. Rohrbaugh. 'A competing values approach to organisational effectiveness'. *Public Productivity Review*, 1981, 122–140.

Integrating the two tensions draws out important implications for specific areas of focus to ensure 'all the bases are covered'. Figure 2.3.4 illustrates the two dynamic tensions, along with the areas of focus relevant to the resulting quadrants that have been shown in scientific research[9] to determine business performance: 'well-being', 'innovation', 'achievement' and 'internal processes'[10].

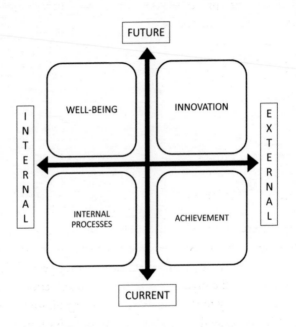

Figure 2.3.4 Managing performance tensions.

---

9 Based on M. Patterson, M. West, R. Lawthon & S. Nickell. *Impact of People Management Practices on Business Performance.* Institute of Personnel and Development: London, 1997.

10 Quinn & Rohrbaugh (1981) originally labelled these as human relations, open systems, rational goals and internal process respectively. These were renamed in G. Jones, M. Gittins & L. Hardy. 'Creating an environment where high performance is inevitable and sustainable: The High Performance Environment Model'. *Annual Review of High Performance Coaching and Consulting,* 2009, 139–149.

- **Achievement** – this current and external focus is about delivering against short-term goals, typically in the form of revenue and profit, that ensures the immediate stability of the organisation. My experience is that there is a huge emphasis and focus on this in the retail sector, where short-term revenue generation is so important.
- **Internal processes** – this current and internal focus is on the internal systems, processes, procedures etc. underpinning the efficiency of organisations. Examples include performance management systems and IT infrastructure. In my experience, government and public agencies have a very strong emphasis and focus on this factor because many of them are typified by the demand to manage a huge amount and flow of information efficiently and accurately.
- **Innovation** – this future and external focus is aimed at securing the longer-term health of the organisation and is largely directed at the marketplace and things like new products and initiatives. The types of organisation I have worked with who have a heavy emphasis on market sector innovation include pharmaceuticals, who try incessantly to develop the next wonder drug.
- **Well-being** – this future and internal focus drives the longer-term sustainability of performance by ensuring people's level of commitment to the organisation, their job satisfaction and their trust in and loyalty to the leadership of the organisation that is so vital to future growth[11]. It also enables organisations to retain their top talent and to grow their own people. Typically, organisations with a rapid growth strategy and where incentives are considerable and based on individual performance have a lesser focus on well-being.

---

11 P. Podsakoff, S. MacKenzie & W. Bommer. 'Transformational leadership behaviours and their effects on followers' trust in leader, satisfaction and organisational citizenship behaviours'. *Journal of Management*, 1996, 259–298.

Of course, it is the relative degree of focus on these factors, and how the levels are balanced against each other, which is important in delivering top performance. The dynamic nature of the tensions means that planned shifts in strategic focus need to be factored into the design process. For example, an organisation in the early stages of change will probably have a heavy focus on internal processes which is planned to diminish as systems become embedded and the focus is directed more towards the other quadrants. External forces will also demand a change in focus, which organisations need to have a plan, or 'what if', for.

The framework described above emanates from work in the business world and I have found it to have a strong impact in helping business leaders and their teams design the strategic focus required to deliver their defined performance. This approach is easily transferred outside the business arena because all organisations in all performance sectors are faced with managing the same tensions; achieving the right balance between current and future focus, and at the same time, ensuring an appropriate focus on what is going on inside and outside of the organisation. It is just the detail that differs.

2.4 Delivering top performance

Of course, the crunch comes when the performance that has been so carefully defined and designed has to be delivered. The definition of performance might be clear and compelling, and the plan might seem bulletproof, but without the delivery capability these are worth no more than the paper they are written on. This is where two types of know-how about delivering performance are important: 1) regulating performance, and 2) balancing effectiveness and efficiency.

Regulating performance

No matter how meticulously performance has been defined and designed, the road to success is seldom totally smooth and there will be points when bumps and sometimes rocks must be negotiated. And occasionally, things go even better than planned, which can potentially be as dangerous as navigating the rocks! In any eventuality the ability to make appropriate adjustments will be necessary and this section outlines some of the key factors to be mindful of when regulating performance, as shown in Figure 2.4.1.

- **Control the crucial controllables.** The classic sound bite in the performance arena is the exhortation to 'control the controllables'. Wise advice, but it does not tell the full story. Some controllables are much more significant than others and the identification of and continuous focus on those 'crucial controllables' is fundamental in enabling the regulation of performance. Employee retention, for example, is a metric of success in many organisations and impressive retention rates are viewed as a sign of engagement and satisfaction and doing a good job of controlling hearts and minds. Regulating performance, however, is dependent on people who possess the ability, mindset and know-how to initiate and/or implement what is required. So the *crucial* controllable that will make the difference is actually retention of the *top* performers.

- **Focus on the processes.** Understanding the processes underpinning performance and how they fit together is crucial to regulating performance when necessary. 'Doing simple things well' is the mantra of many successful leaders, who recognise the need to reduce performance to its core basic processes and principles and to ensure these are practised and carried out effectively. Process input goals were highlighted in Part 2.3 as being particularly important in sport, where performers go to great lengths to monitor progress towards their targets and place a lot of emphasis on measuring processes. It is through these processes that they are able to regulate performance. The best performers and their coaches and other support staff know precisely how they can work towards shaving .02 of a second here and .05 of a second there off their times, and plan meticulously for how to achieve it.

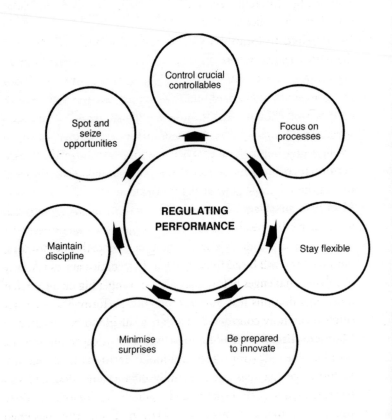

Figure 2.4.1 Regulating performance.

- **Stay flexible.** In some cases, changing performance requires a focus on strategy and tactics and having the flexibility to alter them when necessary. A tennis player, for example, may adopt a serve-and-volley tactic when her baseline game is not having the desired effect. The player will feel comfortable implementing this change since she will have practised and developed both tactics to very high levels. Similarly, a leader should, ideally, feel equally at ease using different styles of leadership to suit particular situations and followers.

- **Be prepared to innovate.** Occasionally, it is necessary to make dramatic changes in order to gain a new perspective on the overall performance plan and strategy. These times often call for bringing about change through innovation. There are numerous examples of extraordinary innovation in the world of top-level sport. I have already described one of the best-known when, in 1968, a high jumper called Dick Fosbury transformed his own performance when he perfected the now-famous 'Fosbury Flop' to win the Olympic gold medal in Mexico.

- **Minimise surprises.** There should not be too many surprises when delivering performance. This is achieved by identifying the things that could deviate from the designed path and working out how they will be addressed; 'what if' scenarios are a great way of solving challenges before they arise. Losing a big client is what most organisations fear, for example, but performance need not suffer if carefully considered plans are available to be executed.

- **Maintain discipline.** Failure to deliver to plan carries with it the obvious risk of panic and irrational decisions and actions. Performance that has been carefully defined and designed will have factored in such scenarios and maintaining discipline at these times is crucial. However, deviation from the designed performance path is not always in the wrong direction. Sometimes, things may be going much better than planned but they do not always have the positive consequences that might be imagined. Getting carried away with success is a potential derailer, that lurks just around the corner from any achievement. My first-hand experience of working with equity traders has taught me that this poses a real danger for them. A string of gains can lead to an air of invincibility and irrational risks, which will eventually result in heavy losses. Maintaining discipline is something that needs to be planned and prepared for in the absence of the pressure associated with performance delivery.

- **Spot and seize opportunities.** The highest achievers in any field are great at spotting and seizing opportunities. They make things happen to stay one step ahead of the competition through clear decision-making which enables the positive momentum to be maintained. However, they are also very careful to ensure they do not compromise longer-term success by short-term gains. Making an acquisition, for example, will have a short-term impact on the growth of an organisation but may present challenges down the line in terms of time, effort and focus required to integrate the different cultures.

Balancing effectiveness and efficiency

The delivery of sustained top performance is driven by a focus on both effectiveness and efficiency – they go hand in hand. However, the short-termism pervading many organisations means that efficiency does not figure as prominently as warranted. This is largely because effectiveness is tangible and can be measured and delivered in a relatively short time frame, whilst efficiency is often more difficult to measure and takes time to achieve, which means it is easy to ignore.

The threat to the sustainability and longevity of top performance posed by this blinkered approach played out clearly in an organisation which I will call 'Anonimus'. A relatively young company in a fast-moving market sector, Anonimus had recently been acquired by a large conglomerate. It had returned impressive performance and growth over the couple of years prior to its acquisition and its new parent company was quick to set it even more challenging growth targets. Anonimus managed to deliver the numbers over the first year, but the targets became even more stretching. My colleagues and I were invited to assist the company in stepping up to yet higher levels of performance.

What we found was a business full of passion, enthusiasm and a hard-work ethic that was struggling to keep up with the unrelenting expectations imposed on it. The company had got by in previous years on the back of the energy that people had devoted to its success. It was effective in delivering performance, but it was not efficient; basic processes such as communication, performance reviews and inter-teamwork were inadequate to sustain the required growth. And the fast pace at which it was operating meant that the organisation had little opportunity to put these processes in place. Anonimus was struggling to meet its targets because whilst it had been effective, it lacked the required efficiency; success had been achieved but at a cost to the energy and motivation of its key employees. Top performance was not sustainable in these circumstances and required efficient processes to underpin it. As shown in Figure 2.4.2, this combination of high effectiveness but low efficiency (1) was providing short-term successes but at an unsustainable cost.

The moral behind the story of Anonimus is quite simple: as shown in Figure 2.4.2, top performance is only sustainable when high effectiveness is underpinned by totally aligned high efficiency (2). Even then, organisations must closely monitor effectiveness and efficiency to ensure their continued balance and alignment. The figure also shows what is likely to happen in the other two sets of circumstances. Where there is high efficiency but low effectiveness (3), the organisation may be characterised by smooth-running units that seldom achieve their targets because of the lack of a performance edge. I have come across one or two companies with highly efficient processes and systems and which are 'nice' places to work, but to the extent where performance issues are never seriously addressed. In others, the issues may be more about the calibre of the performers in that they are simply not competent enough to deliver the required performance despite the processes and systems they have at their disposal. Low efficiency accompanied by low effectiveness (4) presents a serious challenge, where the most sensible option is probably to dismantle and start again!

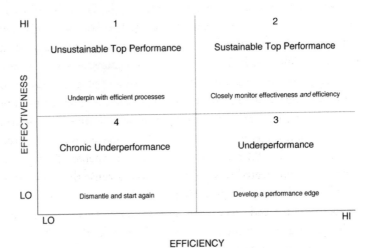

Figure 2.4.2 Balancing effectiveness and efficiency.

The same is true in sport. It has been well documented that the England rugby union team were only able to win the World Cup in 2003 following a total commitment on the part of Sir Clive Woodward[12] to create an environment in which success was eventually inevitable. Woodward left no stone unturned, bringing in specialist support staff to cover the specific areas of expertise that had previously been lacking. He researched what other successful teams did well, both on and off the field, and set out to do it bigger and better. Woodward turned the whole environment in which the England team and its support staff functioned into one that others looked and aspired to; innovation, adaptability and attention to detail were key to their success. His policy of selecting players on the basis of their last performance and not on reputation created a real 'performance edge' and an associated hunger and desire among all concerned. What Woodward did so successfully was to get everyone bought into the vision of winning the 2003 World Cup, whether they were on the field or not. He had created an *efficient* operation with a system of interlocking cogs that worked in unison and would deliver *effectiveness* when it was most required.

There is another 'side' to this story, however, which serves as an important source of learning for all organisations. The fortunes of the England rugby team went rapidly downhill after their World Cup triumph! It seems the intense focus on success was so centred on winning the 2003 event that it was at the expense of longevity. What had been created was not sustainable because there had been insufficient planning for post-2003.

More recently, and more impressive because of its sustainability, has been the achievement of British Cycling under the leadership of Sir Dave Brailsford. Success in three successive Olympics at Athens, Beijing and London has made Team GB the most successful track cycling team in modern history. Brailsford has publicly referred to 'marginal gains' as being a core strategy that has driven performance

---

12 C. Woodward. *Winning*, London: Hodder & Stoughton, 2004.

to new heights. This involves breaking down absolutely everything that could impact on a cycling performance, from fitness to the pillows the cyclists sleep on. Focusing on improving every little thing by 1 per cent is what he says has made the significant performance difference. Focusing on both effectiveness *and* efficiency to stretch performance boundaries is what has underpinned Brailsford's philosophy on leadership, and to great effect.

2.5 Summary

Top performance does not just happen. On the rare occasions when it does, the likelihood of repeating it is small since awareness and understanding of how it was achieved is lacking. Instead, it is the result of a paradigm or process of first clearly *defining* what top performance will look like, whether in the form of a vision or perhaps outputs, outcomes and impacts. Defining how it will be measured is an implicit part of this process and identifying CPIs is, indeed, critical. The *design* phase of the top performance process involves identifying outcome, output and input goals which are totally aligned with the defined performance, as well as getting the strategic focus right in terms of managing the 'current versus future' and 'internal versus external' performance tensions. Of course, the real test of having got the process right lies in the performance *delivery* and this is where the ability to regulate performance and to balance effectiveness and efficiency are key.

Part 3

The Top Performance Environment

Creating the Conditions in Which People Can Thrive

3.1 What does the top performance environment look like?

By now it should be clear that in reality top performance leaders are only ever measured on one thing – performance. Inspiring people to follow them is insufficient to satisfy key stakeholders and keep them in their job if it is not accompanied by performance returns. At the same time, short-term performance gains are no good if they are not deliverable year-in, year-out. This is where the performance environment is critical. Leaders may have great people around them and in the wider organisation but if the environment is not 'right' for them, then they risk either losing them or their performance dropping off. My experience of working with top performers in numerous settings and contexts has taught me about the need to create the conditions where top performers can thrive. Too often, the assumption is made that selecting the best people means that they will achieve under any circumstances. This is not the case, and the crucial lesson is that the performance environment is just as important as the people who operate within it, whether they are top performers, people who aspire to top performance or those who might be struggling to live up to expectations.

This is what drove myself and colleagues to research and identify the essential elements of top performance environments[13], which

13 Part 3 is based on research funded by Knowledge Transfer Partnerships (KTP), a UK government-funded programme to help businesses improve their competitiveness and productivity. This collaboration between Lane4 and University of Wales, Bangor, won one of nine best-project awards in 2007 at a time when more than 1,000 KTP projects were running.

we subsequently published in the peer-reviewed scientific literature. The culminating model has been validated in different performance domains, including business, sport and the military. I will not bore you with the specific detail of the research and, instead, will short-circuit to the core finding that the Top Performance Environment (TPE) includes the four essential elements shown in Figure 3.1.1.[14]

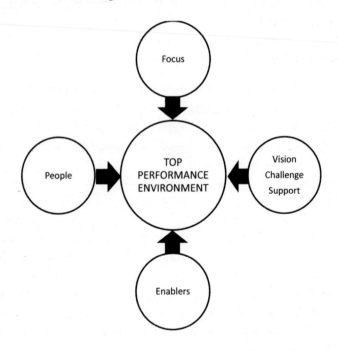

Figure 3.1.1 The Top Performance Environment.

---

14 The research evidence underpinning the identification of these elements and how specific aspects of each of them influence the performance environment can be found in G. Jones, M. Gittins & L. Hardy, 'Creating an environment where high performance is inevitable and sustainable: The High Performance Environment Model'. *Annual Review of High Performance Coaching and Consulting*, 2009, 139–149.

Briefly, these elements comprise:

- Focus – achieving a focus which is aligned with the defined top performance aspirations but also satisfies the needs of those tasked with delivering the performance
- Vision, challenge, support – achieving a balance where people feel stretched but also have the required support offered or available to them
- Enablers – having the tools in place that will help people deliver top performance
- People – having people with the appropriate capacity, mindset and behaviours to deliver the goods

Having worked hard to define and design the top performance aspirations using some or all of the strategies and techniques described in Part 2, top performance leaders then oversee and ensure that all four elements are in place and aligned with those aspirations to constitute the TPE.

I alerted you in the Introduction to the fact that there is a lot to think about as a top performance leader, and also a lot for you to absorb as a reader. This particularly applies to this part of the book, in which various layers of detail are peeled back and revealed. Some of the detail may appear obvious, but it is all too easy for the obvious to be overlooked and taken for granted, which is why it is included here. Nothing must be left to chance in creating a TPE in which people can thrive. Gaps, weaknesses or misalignments in any of the elements will result in an environment that will not be conducive to delivering the performance required.

3.2 Getting the focus right

Where leaders direct their focus is critical because it will send strong signals to their people about what is important and how they should think and behave. The Managing Performance Tensions framework discussed in Part 2.3 described how two dynamic tensions – 'future versus current' and 'internal versus external' – are instrumental in guiding and shaping the strategic focus in organisations. The management of these two tensions and the resulting focus also has enormous implications for the environment people operate within.

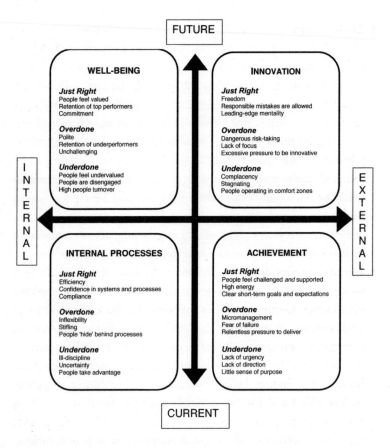

Figure 3.2.1 Focus and the environment.

Figure 3.2.1 shows examples of how getting the focus 'just right' in each of the well-being, innovation, internal processes and achievement areas can impact on the environment. It also shows how directing too much ('overdone') or too little ('underdone') focus in each of the areas can have a detrimental effect on the ensuing environment.

Specifically, the impact of focus in the various areas can influence the performance environment in the following ways:

- **Achievement** – environments dominated by an achievement focus are typically fast-paced, incentives-driven and task-focused. A 'just right' focus on achievement will result in an environment where the short-term goals are clear, there is high energy, people feel stretched but supported and there is a sense of achievement as successes are celebrated. On the other hand, an 'overdone' emphasis on this area is often characterised by micromanagement, relentless demands and pressure to deliver, people operating at the limits of their capability who are at risk of burnout, unhealthy competition, an obsession with 'hitting the numbers' and a fear of the consequences of not doing so. An 'underdone' focus on achievement means that there is a lack of urgency and direction, little sense of purpose and little to celebrate.
- **Internal processes** – environments dominated by an internal processes focus are typically slower-paced and have a big emphasis on accuracy. Getting the focus 'just right' in this area results in an environment characterised by high standards, confidence in systems and processes, efficiency, compliance and risk awareness. An 'overdone' focus results in confusion, risk-aversion, excessive bureaucracy, hiding behind processes, inflexibility and people feeling stifled and frustrated. An 'underdone' focus will result in poor or inappropriate systems and processes which, in turn, leads to chaos, uncertainty, ill-discipline and the risk of people making the rules up as they go along to take advantage in a self-serving way.

- **Innovation** – organisations dominated by a focus on innovation typically have environments characterised by risk-taking, space for creative thinking and energy. A 'just right' focus on innovation will result in an environment where people have a sense of relative freedom and discretion, responsible mistakes are allowed, there is a high level of expectant energy and a leading-edge mentality. On the other hand, an 'overdone' emphasis on this area is often characterised by a lack of focus, dangerous risk-taking and excessive pressure to be innovative, driven by a fear of losing competitive advantage. An 'underdone' focus on innovation can cause complacency and stagnation with people operating within their comfort zones and who are uninspired doing what they have always done.

- **Well-being** – environments dominated by an emphasis on well-being typically focus on employee engagement, retention, benefits, surveys and people development initiatives. Getting the focus 'just right' in this area results in an environment where people feel valued, supported and listened to. Commitment, loyalty and collaboration are high, as is the retention rate of the top performers. An 'overdone' focus in this area results in a polite, unchallenging environment with the risk that people are not stretched and things are too cosy. An 'overdone' focus on well-being may also mean that mistakes are overlooked and underperformance is not addressed, so that underperformers remain whilst disgruntled top performers leave. An 'underdone' focus on well-being can result in people feeling undervalued, disengaged and potentially stressed due to the lack of attention and support. Turnover is likely to be high in these circumstances.

The challenge for leaders is to ensure that the balance of focus is just right to deliver the defined top performance *and* create a productive environment at the same time. Leaders in organisations focused on short-term rapid growth must ensure that this does not have a deleterious effect on well-being. Where there is a major focus on and investment in the long-term, leaders must create an environment that accommodates their top performers' need to achieve via a complementary focus on the short-term. Whatever the circumstances and aspirations, having an appropriate focus on all four areas – 'covering all the bases' – is essential.

3.3 Getting the vision, challenge and support balance right

Leaders have a big influence on the environment surrounding them and sometimes in ways they will never know. A smile here, a frown there, a sign of impatience, a problem unaddressed, a closed office door, a curt email, an absence from a meeting, and so on will all be interpreted in ways that get talked about and the ensuing stories reinforce and perpetuate the environment they may have inadvertently or subconsciously created. Top performance leaders recognise and use this 'power' to shape the environment that they have already identified as being required to deliver the top performance they have so carefully defined and designed.

An essential element of top performance leaders' conscious shaping of TPEs is their use and role modelling of three key drivers of top performance – vision, challenge and support – and getting the right balance between them. Get it wrong and the result will be an environment that is highly unlikely to deliver top performance. I have seen this happen so many times in organisations where people feel they have 'been given' unachievable targets and left on their own to hit them. Less common, but equally detrimental to the performance environment, are organisations in which people have told me they feel unchallenged and that too much investment has been made in unnecessary support functions and processes.

Vision, challenge and support can take on various guises depending on the specific context and performance aspirations. In its simplest form, providing **vision** involves reminding people of the clearly defined performance expectations, and when it is due to be delivered. This reinforcement of where the organisation, department or team is headed serves as a continual reminder of everyone's purpose and provides direction and cohesion. It reinforces the collective commitment, responsibility and 'in it together' mentality necessary across the organisation. Reminding people of the vision is particularly important when things are not going so well or where they might be struggling. Athletes who have training days when nothing goes right, for example, may need to recall their long-term goal – perhaps that gold medal or number one status – to get them back on track by reminding themselves what the hard work and setbacks are about and why they must endure them, learn from them and come back stronger.

Words alone, however, will not have any enduring influence on the performance environment. Actions and, crucially, role modelling are the things that will make the difference. As described in Part 2.1, telling detailed stories of how the environment will look and feel on the journey to achieving the vision inspires an excitement that quickly spreads, as people conjure up their own aspirations of what it will mean for them. Regular updates on progress towards the vision are a simple means of shaping the environment by keeping the carefully defined performance at the forefront of people's minds. And, as described in Part 2.4, the demise of the England rugby team after their 2003 World Cup success is a clear indicator of the importance of identifying what lies beyond the vision as it gets closer.

Challenge involves stretching and stimulating people to deliver their contribution to achieving the vision by finding ways of continually developing and improving their performance. It can take many forms, some of them more constructive than others! Challenge behaviours exhibited by leaders in TPEs include reinforcing their high performance expectations and challenging people to think about old problems and issues in new ways. Providing developmental feedback on areas for improving competence is a powerful tool for instilling accountability and responsibility. Challenge is about moving people out of their comfort zones and opening them to experiences that will test and develop their capabilities. Through appropriate challenge, leaders communicate performance excellence, set stretching goals and foster innovation and adaptability.

However, challenge without **support** creates a 'sink or swim' environment in which people are left to their own devices with the risk of floundering in silence. Providing support in helping them deliver their contribution is therefore critical in sustaining a TPE. Through appropriate support, leaders promote learning and build trust among their respective followers. People in TPEs are told when they are doing a good job: motivational feedback in the form of encouragement supports them in reinforcing what is expected of them and helps to maintain their confidence and motivation. Top performance leaders know their people as individuals and provide them with the specific individual support they need; taking a personal interest in them earns considerable loyalty and commitment among them.

The optimal vision, challenge and support balance will be determined by specific contexts and aspirations; however, the principle that all three are required to create a TPE stands across all performance domains. But what are the consequences when the three behaviours are *not* all present? Figure 3.3.1 shows the possible permutations ranging from all three being high to those scenarios where one or two are low and the likely resulting environment.

Vision	Challenge	Support	Environment is ...
√	√	√	Top performance
√	√	X	Sink or swim
√	X	X	Pipe-dream
√	X	√	Cosy
X	X	√	Polite
X	√	X	Urgent
X	√	√	Rudderless
X	X	X	Stagnant

√ =High   X = Low

Figure 3.3.1 Vision, challenge, support and the environment.[15]

Some of the likely characteristics of the environments created by the various combinations of vision, challenge and support provided by leaders are described below:

Top performance:

- Vision, challenge and support are all evident and appropriately balanced, resulting in high levels of supportive challenge towards a clearly defined vision
- Individuals and teams are clear as to what is expected of them on a day-to-day basis, as well as in the longer-term
- Success is recognised and celebrated
- Coaching is the norm, being underpinned by good working relationships, a feedback culture, accountability and ownership, and clearly defined goals
- There is a 'we're in it together' mentality that is the foundation of top-performing teams

---

15 Adapted from G. Jones (2010).

- 'Healthy competition' exists in the form of shared learning and commitment to everyone's development, as well as individual and team goals being completely aligned

Sink or swim:

- Individuals and teams are continually reminded of the vision and there is plenty of challenge to deliver it, but little support
- The lack of support accompanied by high challenge results in a 'sink or swim' environment which breeds an 'I'm on my own' as well as 'out to impress' mentality
- Top performance is possible but probably not sustainable because of stress and potential burnout
- There is likely to be a blame culture, which becomes evident when the high standards are not achieved
- Recognition for good performance is likely to be rare because it is expected
- There is little care for well-being, resulting in many people feeling uncomfortable and under the spotlight

Pipe-dream:

- The vision is talked about regularly but is nothing more than a pipe-dream because of the lack of challenge and support
- There are no plans in place for how the vision will be achieved
- The leader lacks credibility
- There is a lack of goals so that individuals are unclear about expectations
- The culture is one of mediocrity
- There is an 'I don't know what I'm supposed to be doing' mentality

Cosy:

- There is a vision and plenty of support available, but little in the way of challenge
- Underperformance is not addressed
- It is too cosy and individuals are working within their comfort zones
- There is little sense and celebration of achievement because it is not valued highly
- It can be stifling for individuals who want to be stretched
- There is an 'out to please' mentality

Polite:

- Lack of vision and challenge means there is no direction
- The high support and the absence of challenge can create an overly caring, parent-like culture
- Ambiguity and uncertainty abound because individuals are unsure what is expected of them in the short-term, and they are also unsure where they are headed
- There is an air of complacency
- People are bored
- There is an 'I'm safe as long as I keep my head down' mentality

Urgent:

- Pressure is high because the emphasis on short-term performance is combined with the lack of support and a vision
- There is potential conflict among individuals and teams because of the short-term urgency to produce results
- People do not feel valued because they are unsure how the performance demanded from them contributes to the future of the organisation

- The short-term performance focus results in micromanagement
- 'Unhealthy competition' exists in the form of a lack of willingness to work effectively in teams because the 'big picture' is unclear, there is a failure to share best practice and a focus on 'beating' your colleagues
- An 'avoidance' mentality exists because of the consequences of failing or making mistakes

Rudderless:

- There is lots of challenge and support, but nobody knows what the vision is
- Focus is on short-term performance, but the pressure is alleviated by the high support that is available
- High challenge and high support results in a focus on inspiring people to deliver more
- The culture is one of 'busyness'; there is plenty going on
- Silos exist because the lack of a vision means that teams do not have an overt reason for working together effectively
- There is an 'I'm not sure why I'm working so hard' mentality

Stagnant:

- There appears to be little going on; it is a stagnating environment
- There is a strong sense of politics
- It is more about *who* you know than *what* you know
- People are not stimulated
- A lot happens behind closed doors
- There is little respect for the leaders
- Good performance happens more by accident than by design
- There is an 'I don't care' mentality

The critical point is that environments not conducive to top performance are created by leaders who anchor themselves in one or two areas to the exclusion of the other(s). The undesirable impact on the performance environment of the various imbalances across vision, challenge and support clearly demonstrates the importance of focusing on and practising all three behaviours. Creating a TPE where top performance is inevitable and sustainable is an unrealistic goal unless all three behaviours are clearly and consistently evident. Focusing on demonstrating vision, challenge and support behaviours can inspire extraordinary performance from people who not only surprise their leader, but also themselves.

3.4 Getting the enablers in place that will help people deliver top performance

It was several years ago when I went to the Albert Hall in London to watch the Cirque du Soleil for the first time. What a jaw-dropping and breathtaking experience! Amazing feats of acrobatics involving strength, coordination and artistic creativity which mere mortals like you and I can only wonder at, came together to produce a show that was totally enthralling and mesmerising. I am sure you have had similar experiences yourself. Perhaps it was a stage play, opera or ballet, or maybe you were watching and listening to a leading orchestra or band playing your favourite piece of music. Whatever the performance you were witnessing, think about what would have been happening behind the scenes, before and during, to enable that performance to happen.

Performances like those described above do not just happen; they are the end product of a multitude of enablers that come together to deliver something extraordinary time and again. Practice, preparation, training, choreography, scripting, artistry, timing and technology are just a few of the more obvious enablers; there will be numerous others beyond the comprehension of the naïve eye. That is what is so important about enablers and top performance; there are so many of them and all must be identified, maximised and made to synchronise in a manner that produces seamless top performance, time and again.

In order to reduce the task of identifying performance enablers to manageable proportions, and in a form that is applicable and transferable across all performance domains, they can be thought of in the context of creating a TPE that comprises three 'types' of enabler, shown in Figure 3.4.1, that people are **provided with and have access to.**

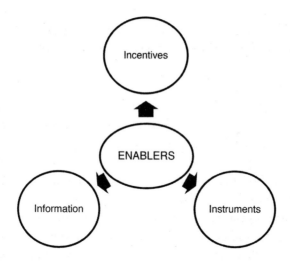

Figure 3.4.1 Getting the enablers in place.

Specifically:

• 'Incentives' enable people to motivate themselves to deliver their best

- 'Information' enables people to be clear about what is expected of them and how to perform their role
- 'Instruments' enable people in the form of having the appropriate tools to help them perform

Incentives

The ideal performance environment would include people who are all optimally motivated to deliver top performance at all times without incentives. Alas, such an environment does not exist and people need things to be in place so that they are able to motivate themselves. The reference to 'motivate themselves' is critical; an environment where people are dependent on the organisation or leader to motivate them will not deliver top performance, at least at a sustainable level. Top performance leaders do not motivate people as such; they create an environment where people feel intrinsically motivated.

Motivation is a complex concept and there are numerous theories and concepts that you can read about if you have the time and inclination. If not, then I will help you by short-circuiting to the seminal work on motivation in the form of Self-Determination Theory (SDT) by Richard Ryan and Edward Deci[16]. Their work identified three innate needs that, if satisfied, foster well-being and allow optimal function and growth: competence, autonomy and relatedness. An important underlying assumption is that humans have an inherent tendency towards growth development and actions but they do not happen automatically. Essentially, in order to actualise their inherent potential, people need nurturing from the environment[17].

---

16 R. Ryan & E. Deci. 'Self-determination theory and the facilitation of intrinsic motivation, social development and well-being'. *American Psychologist*, 2000, 68–78.
17 E. Deci & M. Vansteenkiste. 'Self-determination theory and basic need satisfaction: Understanding human development in positive psychology'. *Ricerche di Psichologia*, 2004, 17–34.

This is where the environment leaders create and shape becomes ever more critical; the conditions need to be in place where people can self-actualise. This underpins the earlier premise that 'top performance leadership involves creating the conditions for people to thrive'. These conditions involve satisfying people's needs and this is where leaders can get it wrong. Figure 3.4.2 shows how the people's needs and the organisation's or leader's needs can exist at opposite ends of a continuum, meaning both parties' needs cannot be satisfied at the same time. Consequently, goals and objectives are sometimes set with only the organisation's needs in mind. Incessant reminders about hitting numbers and targets are only ever likely to satisfy the organisation's needs and people can quickly feel as if they themselves are 'a number' in organisations where short-termism prevails. Finding ways of satisfying people's *and* the organisation's needs at the same time is key to creating a TPE where people's engagement and commitment is high and sustained.

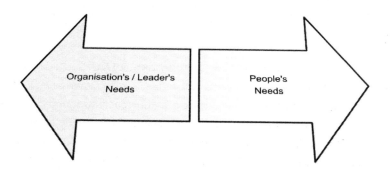

Figure 3.4.2 The challenge of satisfying the organisation's, leader's *and* the people's needs

This is where SDT can provide a way forward. As described earlier, SDT states that people thrive and have the best chance of achieving their potential when their needs for competence, autonomy and relatedness are satisfied. But how can the environment be shaped to satisfy them?

Competence. People generally want to feel good about themselves and since they spend the majority of their waking existence at work, the organisation's environment, and especially leaders within it, are important determinants of how they do feel about themselves. Organisations generally place a heavy emphasis on salaries, bonuses and benefits as a means of rewarding competence. However, this is only one dimension of incentives and neglects the day-to-day ways of satisfying this need. Praise, attention and recognition for good performance, especially when unexpected,[18] are important means of enhancing perceptions of competence, when authentic and warranted, of course. Providing opportunities for personal and functional development and furthering their career is a means of satisfying people's longer-term need for competence, whilst setting short-term goals that are monitored and updated regularly is an easily incorporated way of allowing people to gauge their competence on an ongoing basis.

Autonomy. People generally want to feel that they have control over their destiny and daily existence so that satisfying the need for autonomy essentially involves providing them with perceived choices. Coaching as a leadership tool is especially powerful in getting people to assume the responsibility that necessitates making choices about many aspects of delivering performance. Asking questions, in particular, is a good way of instilling a sense of autonomy in people. An environment where people feel empowered is one that satisfies this need and this is where the leader is so important in shaping it. Their willingness to let go,

---

18 E. Deci. 'Effects of externally mediated rewards on intrinsic motivation'. *Journal of Personality and Social Psychology*, 1971, 105–115.

delegate and suppress an urge to provide answers because it is quicker and easier are all required if this is to be sustainable.

Relatedness. This is about people's need to interact and have a sense of belonging. The need is often satisfied in an environment where there are strong relationships with line managers and leaders so that communication is open, honest and frequent. Being involved in decision-making helps to enhance people's sense of influencing the wider organisation and their need for relatedness. Importantly, satisfying the need for relatedness helps in providing them with a sense of *meaning* to their existence, in terms of how their individual roles contribute to the greater good of the organisation and its cause.

Satisfying all three needs is fundamental to creating an environment where people can thrive and perform at their best. They bring with them an energy and vibrancy missing in environments where they are not satisfied and people are just 'going through the motions'.

Information

Information is a fundamental enabler that is so easy to get wrong. And it can be so 'obvious' that it is sometimes taken for granted and overlooked. Not long ago, I had an experience that made me realise just how important even the most basic information is in influencing the performance environment. I was on holiday and had worked hard to stick to my pre-holiday commitment to exercise in the gym every other day. The beginning of my first workout had been delayed by frustration that I could not get the console to work on the gym's sole rowing machine. After several minutes of tinkering, the gym attendant approached me with the news that the machine was awaiting repair and that it would be several days before it would be back in proper working order.

Working out on a rowing machine was an important goal and so I pressed on regardless, using only the clock on the wall to inform me of my progress. On the second visit to the gym, I noticed that my drive to perform on the rowing machine was not at its normal level and whilst I rowed for the allotted time, again using only the clock on the wall as a frame of reference, I struggled to push myself. My third and fourth visits were a similar struggle and when I entered the gym for the fifth session I looked at the rowing machine and noticed my motivation to work out on it had almost disappeared. Devoid of any external information, other than duration, on the various aspects of performance such as calories burned, reps per minute and distance travelled, my motivation to exert effort had waned over the sessions to the point where I now gave up and decided to work out on the cross trainer instead.

Here began the second part of my experience, which drove home the importance of the most basic information in creating TPEs. I am not what might be called an 'experienced' user of cross trainers and this particular machine was a model I had never seen before. I looked at the console and was so confused by the large array of buttons that I could not even figure how to turn it on. Flustered, and in a busy gym with what I perceived to be lots of experienced users, my embarrassment got the better of me and I was not about to call for the gym attendant's help. I got off the cross trainer and did some stretching instead.

Emerging from my experiences in the gym are two key messages about information as a performance enabler and how it shapes the performance environment:

1. People need fundamental information on how to perform their roles. Without this basic information, they do not know where to start and will flounder, often to the extent where they feel embarrassed to ask for support.

2. People need information on their performance so they can monitor progress and use it to set goals for themselves. If this information is absent or slow to be delivered, or of poor quality, then their motivation and effort will gradually reduce to the point where they may even stop trying.

Fundamental to the environment where top performance is inevitable and sustainable, therefore, is the information provided to people about how to perform their role effectively and how it will be evaluated, as well as continual information, or performance feedback, on how they are progressing. People also want to know how they can progress through the organisation and will require developmental feedback and clear goals that they have been involved in setting along the way. They should also be clear about how the effective performance of their role contributes to the organisational aspirations, as well as having clarity about the expectations and scope of their responsibilities and the behaviours required to fulfil them. All of these factors give employees a sense of meaning and structure within their performance environment.

In a TPE, people also receive regular information on how the organisation as a whole, as well as other parts, is performing. Top performance leaders spend time reflecting on the information their people want and need to know – the successes, setbacks, changes, innovations etc. In a TPE people know a lot about the organisation as a whole and not just their specific part.

Senior leaders in TPEs also devote careful consideration and time to identifying what their 'non-negotiables' are. This is a critical part of top performance leadership and is information that will have a big impact on shaping the environment. Only two or three non-negotiables are needed but they must be clearly thought through, linked to the organisation's CPIs described in Part 2, be crystal clear and be continually reinforced throughout the organisation, department or team. Leaders' non-negotiables will of course be specific to the defined performance aspirations, but typical exemplars at the wider organisational level include things such as not compromising safety in a construction business and total commitment to quality within a healthcare organisation.

Instruments

The final enabler exists in the form of instruments that are essentially the tools that people are provided with and have access to in order to help them deliver top individual and collective performances. In some environments the absence, obsoletion or under-resourcing of instruments can, quite literally, be life-threatening. Well-documented stories exist, for example, of how British helicopters operating during the Iraq War were not equipped with a basic infrared device to allow pilots to see at night – a piece of Vietnam-era kit – which resulted in the deaths of several British troops. During the same war, there were widespread reports of British troops being sent into battle without proper protection from chemical or biological attack during a conflict stimulated by fear of President Saddam Hussein's ability to employ such tactics. Soldiers were reportedly issued with dangerously ill-fitting protective suits and respirators and detection alarms that did not work. Furthermore, tanks and armoured vehicles were never fitted with special air filters to protect their crews from such attacks. And thousands of troops were without even the most basic equipment, in the form of desert clothing and boots. A few years later, a Ministry of Defence survey across the Army, Royal Navy and Royal Air Force[19] found that fewer than a third of more than 10,500

---

19 Reported in Mail Online. *'Defence chiefs rocked by a crisis in morale after MOD surveys 10,000 troops'*, 9 August 2009.

military personnel were satisfied with the equipment at their disposal on the front line.

Here is an extreme example where, in these circumstances, an unacceptable lack of appropriate equipment can have deadly consequences. Important for the purpose of the discussion here is that more than half of those surveyed reported morale as being low. The message is loud and clear: the instruments provided and which people have access to will impact on critical aspects of the environment and ensuing performance.

Instruments are clearly specific to different performance arenas and even individual organisations and the sub-units and specialist areas within them. Despite the specialist nature of instruments, it is possible to achieve a level of general applicability by grouping them into three categories:

- **Physical** instruments in the form of tools, technology and equipment, essentially at the core of the dissatisfaction expressed in the MOD survey. At the very least, physical instruments, in whatever shape or form (e.g. work space, video conferencing facilities), need to be fit for purpose. However, giving them higher priority will ensure that the organisation has the best and latest available, enabling them to gain a competitive advantage and demonstrating a genuine commitment to creating the environment where people can thrive and deliver top performance.
- **Knowledge-related** instruments include things like training in new and state-of-the-art systems and processes. There is no point in having the best physical equipment available and then having insufficient people who are trained and developed to put them to their best use. People-development initiatives in the form of things like leadership, teamwork and coaching skills programmes are another type of instrument that will facilitate the delivery of top performance that is sustainable.

- **Structural** instruments comprise things like communication networks (e.g. IT networks, email), the way teams are structured, lines of reporting, performance management systems and processes, focus groups and access to leaders. These underpin the day-to-day ways of working.

The MOD survey findings described earlier demonstrate how the instruments people have access to can have a crucial impact on morale. What the organisation and its leaders are seen to invest its money in will send signals to its people regarding how serious they are about achieving the vision. Having lots of expensive office chairs to sit on when working with outdated computers and software, or cutting leadership-development programme costs whilst emphasising and encouraging a focus on the future, will send contradictory and confusing messages that only serve to create an uncertainty in the environment and distract people from delivering top performance.

Getting the instruments in place that help people deliver top performance requires consulting with those at the coalface about their current and future needs. This process aids morale, but also ensures the instruments provide maximum support and do not get in the way. Instruments should be enablers, not constraints! For example, too much form-filling in the performance appraisal process or other unnecessary time-consuming processes will gradually erode the energy and focus leaders have worked hard to create.

3.5 Getting people to deliver the goods

Having got the strategic focus right, established the appropriate balance across vision, challenge and support, and clarified the enablers that need to be in place, the spotlight moves specifically to the people and leaders' responsibility to get them to deliver the goods. Getting this final piece of the environmental jigsaw right can be a tough challenge for leaders because it necessitates their own recognition and acceptance that they are no longer *real* performers. Their days involved in the detail with sleeves rolled up have gone; now their primary task is to now create the conditions in which those who *are* delivering the performance are able to thrive. Top performance leaders ensure that carefully selected performers with a variety of talents and skills appropriate to the different roles they are playing feel inspired to produce the clearly defined and communicated outcome. They ensure synchrony and a collective commitment to producing the best performance possible, day after day.

Ultimately, it is down to the people and their willingness and ability to deliver the goods. This is where the challenge becomes even tougher because it will require some courage on the leader's part to let go and have the confidence and trust in their people to deliver. Defining and being clear about three areas of expectations and requirements of people will help the leader achieve this and will, at the same time, create the environment that will deliver top performance. The three areas, shown in Figure 3.5.1, are capacity, mindset and behaviours.

Specifically:

- **Capacity** refers to their ability to deliver the required outputs
- **Mindset** reflects their attitudes, beliefs and willingness to perform at their best
- **Behaviours** represent what they do to demonstrate their willingness and ability to perform at their best

Not surprisingly, there are strong links between the three areas. Behaviours are the observable output of the other two and, as such, the only really clear indication of whether people are living up to expectations. For behaviours to meet those expectations, the appropriate capacity and mindset must exist at high levels. Think what would happen if either was low or absent; the environment would either have people who are great at what they do but do not care about the organisation, or those who are committed to the organisation but unable to deliver. So, nurturing people's capacity alongside their mindset is critical if leaders are to witness and enjoy behaviours underpinning an environment that will deliver their performance aspirations.

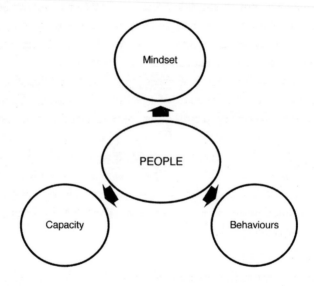

Figure 3.5.1 Getting people to deliver the goods.

Capacity

Capacity can be divided into two aspects which determine how well and effectively people perform their role:

1. A blend of knowledge, experience and technical capabilities appropriate to the role being performed.

2. The 'softer' elements such as their ability to perform under pressure, recover from setbacks and work as part of a team. Resilience, confidence and emotional intelligence are all important assets.

Top performance leaders ensure the recruitment and development of individuals with not only the necessary ability but also the required self-awareness and regulation skills to perform their roles. Top performance is not sustainable if the environment includes people who are brilliant at what they do but fold under the first sign of pressure, or who lack the basic social skills to interact effectively and harmoniously with colleagues. Talent identification and development in both aspects of capacity is always a high priority in TPEs, not just to ensure the individual's continual growth but also to retain them, as well as attracting other top performers from outside the organisation.

Mindset

Research evidence identifies the importance of a number of different dimensions of people's attitudes and beliefs in TPEs, with the key ones being:

- Trust in the leaders
- Commitment to the organisation
- Satisfaction with their roles
- Perceived fit between personal and organisational values
- Collective belief

These are not mutually exclusive, of course, and *trust in the leaders* is particularly important in determining other attitudes and beliefs. It is one of the main reasons why people perform beyond expectations, as well as being strongly linked to high levels of role satisfaction and organisational commitment. *Organisational commitment* is important because it drives increased levels of effort and feelings of personal competence. People's level of *satisfaction* with their role is associated with higher levels of performance, as is the *values fit* between individuals and the organisation. Finally, the *collective belief* of teams and groups is one of the most important characteristics of TPEs. It is associated with higher levels of performance, job satisfaction, organisational commitment, effort and also persistence in the face of problems and setbacks.

Top performance leaders gain their people's trust because it is such an influential factor in shaping the mindsets and commitment of those around them. It engenders an openness underpinning good working relationships where honest feedback and mutual accountability drive top performance.

Behaviours

As indicated earlier, behaviours are the observable output of people's capacity combined with their mindset and, as such, are the only really clear indication of whether people are living up to the leader's expectations. The specific behaviours required will, of course, be dependent on the aspects of the performance environment identified earlier in the process of creating it, particularly the top performance aspirations and associated time frame and strategic focus. It is difficult to generalise, therefore, but research evidence does point towards three key behaviours that are particularly important in organisations where there are TPEs:

- Extra-role
- Role engagement
- Teamwork

Specifically, in TPEs people go beyond their role requirements for the benefit of the organisation; for example, helping colleagues from other teams, and participating voluntarily in work groups and meetings across the organisation. People also demonstrate high levels of engagement with their roles, characterised by high levels of energy, dedication and absorption in their day-to-day work. Finally, teams are very good at cooperating with each other on tasks and coordinating them so that they run smoothly and communicate effectively.

Numerous other behaviours are characteristic of TPEs, including delegation, empowerment, healthy competition, taking ownership and coaching. However, it is their strength in extra-role, role engagement and teamwork behaviours that are especially significant in distinguishing them from lesser-performing environments.

Top performance leaders are clear about the behaviours they expect from their people and quick to recognise and endorse them; they are also quick to address behaviours that are not in line or jeopardise the TPE they have created. Particularly important is their awareness that they are continuously under the spotlight and that their role modelling has a big impact on their people's behaviours.

3.6 Summary

Most organisations are likely to claim that they aspire to creating TPEs, but relatively few have the insight to know what it takes and where to begin, whilst others lack the necessary commitment and perseverance to stick with what can seem like a very daunting challenge. The sheer volume of obvious and not so obvious components, elements and layers of detail that have been covered and which must be factored into any intent to create a TPE demonstrate just how challenging it can be.

The four essential elements of the TPE described here provide an invaluable starting point and tool for diagnosing areas of strength and development requirements within organisations, departments and even teams. Its holistic perspective will enable those leaders facing myriad issues that may appear unrelated to piece them together in a big picture that drives a coordinated approach to developing the whole organisation. The principles are the same in all organisations; it is only the detail that will differ. The mindset, capacity and behaviours required of people in an organisation striving for rapid and hefty growth in their sales revenue, for example, will differ significantly from an organisation focused on delivering the highest-quality healthcare.

Whatever leaders' aspirations are for their organisations, departments or teams, working through the four essential elements when defining and creating the environment will put them in the best possible position to deliver them. Getting the strategic focus right is an important starting point, but remember, it is a dynamic process and will need to be revisited regularly. Also remember, the role of a leader in modelling challenge *and* support is critical for top performance since it is instrumental in setting the day-to-day tone of the environment. And even the best performers will not perform at their best, at least not consistently, without appropriate enablers, so leaders must ensure they have access to them. Finally, leaders must remind themselves that they are no longer 'doing' the performance; their role is to ensure that the people with the right capacity, mindset and behaviours are in place to deliver the goods.

Part 4

Being a Top Performance Leader

Ensuring the Delivery of Sustainable Top Performance

4.1 The essence of being a top performance leader

As I stated at the outset of this book, there is plenty of advice available across a wide range of media on what to do as a leader. In fact, it is the vast and wide-ranging number of things that leaders are apparently expected to be good at and do that can make the role seem complex and at times overwhelming. This book is based on the simple PEL Model: get the definition of top performance right, identify the critical aspects of the environment required to deliver top performance, and then lead accordingly.

Top performance leadership is not about skills and abilities as such, but much more about:

- The *motives* that lie at the core of leaders and which drive their focus, behaviour and intent
- The *support* they are able to attract and harness from those closest to them in terms of their immediate external environment
- The *know-how* they bring or develop as a leader, in terms of how to get the best out of themselves and the broader external environment, which they are able to draw on to sustain themselves

The motives, support and know-how top performance leaders possess are portrayed in Figure 4.1.1 in the form of Real Leadership, Team Leadership and Sustainable Leadership respectively. Real Leadership is about what lies at their core: their drivers, values and beliefs. These are the motives that drive a *real* rather than a *safe* leadership approach. Team Leadership is about their immediate external environment and leading the team of people closest to them. It involves harnessing, inspiring, uniting and aligning those with different skills, abilities, personalities, egos, strengths and weaknesses. Sustainable Leadership is about top performance leaders' stamina, resilience and durability, resulting from use of their know-how and wisdom; this is the interface between their inner self and how they shape and navigate their external environment.

Being a top performance leader requires practising all three types of leadership. Of course, all three are subject to modification and shaping as determined by the specific aspects of the performance environment, which have been identified to deliver the top performance defined at the outset. However, there are some fundamentals underpinning each of them which are applicable across all top performance leaders, and which are described in the sections that follow.

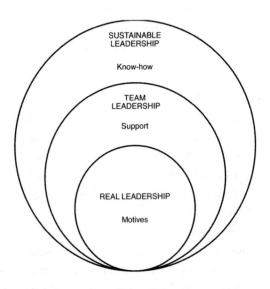

Figure 4.1.1 The essence of being a top performance leader.

4.2 Real leadership

Have you ever considered why leaders choose to be leaders? Is it all about the status, package, power and authority that comes with the role, or is it the responsibility, accountability and vision required that attracts them? Is it about the opportunity to make a difference and have a real impact? My experience of coaching and working with numerous senior leaders across a wide array of organisations has led to my realisation that there are two broad sets of motives for being a leader that drive different behaviours and lead to different impacts on organisations. I have consequently identified two types of leader, which I call 'real' and 'safe' and which exist on a continuum.

Real and *Safe* leaders

At one extreme, *safe* leaders are driven so much by the need for rewards, status and power that they are unwilling to put themselves on the line because of the threat of losing their position if they get it wrong. *Safe* leaders keep their heads out of the firing line, they are risk-averse and there is little or no innovation and challenging orthodoxy during their tenure since their focus is almost exclusively on micro managing the short-term.

At the other extreme, *real* leaders are driven much more by the challenge and opportunity to put themselves out there and make a difference. For them, this is what leadership is about. *Real* leaders are highly visible and make things happen. Their focus is much more on the future and the opportunities that lie ahead. They encourage challenge, innovation and risk-taking, as well as tackling hard issues as soon as they arise.

This distinction has been apparent to me across all market conditions, and some of the key differences between *safe* and *real* leaders that I have noticed and encountered at the extremes of the continuum are shown in Figure 4.2.1.

Safe Leaders	*Real* Leaders
• Are driven by the need for rewards, status and power and are therefore unwilling to put themselves on the line because of the threat of losing their position if they get it wrong	• Are driven much more by the challenge and opportunity to put themselves out there and make a difference; for them, this is what leadership is about
• Focus on tasks	• Focus on people
• Focus on 'what to do' to ensure they conform to company practices and procedures	• Focus on 'how to be' so that they provide good role models for their people
• Rarely innovate or challenge orthodoxy during their tenure because their focus is almost exclusively on micromanaging the short-term	• Empower others to focus on managing the short-term challenges so that their own minds can be more on innovating and investing in the future
• React mainly to immediate day-to-day ongoing issues, claiming that they are too busy to focus on the future	• Create a road map for the future
• Are reluctant to be under the spotlight	• Accept that they are highly visible
• Are reluctant to receive feedback that highlights areas for improvement	• Are hungry for feedback that helps them develop
• Are fearful of making mistakes because of the implications these might have for their job security	• See mistakes as a key part of their development and learning
• Respond to failure by sweeping it under the carpet	• Are courageous in seeking to understand the causes of failure
• View challenge as unhelpful and threatening	• Encourage challenge and collective problem-solving
• Hide behind bureaucracy	• Are willing to take calculated risks to reach stretching goals
• Hide behind resource / capacity constraints	• Create innovative opportunities
• Encourage conformity to 'tried and tested' methods	• Encourage people to challenge accepted ways of thinking and acting
• Dismiss others' suggestions for change	• Cultivate creativity
• Pay lip service to change initiatives	• Lead by example through driving change
• Insist on their people's compliance	• Inspire their people's commitment
• Avoid dealing with the real issues	• Tackle issues head-on
• Are reluctant and slow to tackle underperformance	• Address underperformance when it arises
• Do not challenge or question those in positions of authority	• Ask the difficult questions of those above
• Wait to see what the majority think before speaking up	• Let people know what they think, irrespective of others' views
• Claim a 'messenger' role in communicating tough decisions	• Make and own tough decisions
• Are out to please everyone	• Are willing to make decisions that they know will be unpopular

Figure 4.2.1 Key differences between *Safe* and *Real* leaders.[20]

---

20 From G. Jones. *Thrive on Pressure: Lead and Succeed When Times Get Tough.* McGraw-Hill; New York, 2010.

Of course, *safe* leaders exist in various guises so that different people will exhibit the traits in varying degrees. What is common to them all is their reluctance to put themselves on the line: they have too much to lose if they get it wrong. Some examples of *safe* leaders are as follows:

- I worked with one *safe* leader whose 'motive' was noticeable by his resistance to identify a vision and a long-term strategy and plan for the organisation he headed up. He chose, instead, to keep himself busy by reacting to the usual day-to-day 'trivia', which kept him out of any firing line.
- In another case, a business unit head clearly hid behind an overt claim that her style was to lead through consensus. This led to too much debate and conflict among her team of opinionated, strong-willed and competitive individuals. She was too slow to make the decisions that needed to be made; she was playing it safe.
- Another *safe* leader of a large team lacked the courage to address underperformance. This was mainly underpinned by his need to be liked, and his desire to please everyone around him meant that he claimed to be playing a 'messenger' role in communicating any tough decisions.

Real leaders also come in different 'shapes and sizes'. Some examples are:

- One female managing director of a large distribution company was very clear about her non-negotiables when it came to providing quality customer service. This meant introducing metrics which would highlight areas of weakness and be unpopular with some of her people because they were at risk of being exposed as underperformers. And not all members of her Board agreed with her either, but she was resolute in her rationale and the new metrics resulted in a significant impact on customer satisfaction. Here was a *real* leader who was willing to challenge the status quo despite the fact it was not popular to begin with.

- A leader in a well-known company was instrumental in bringing about a much-needed culture change in the organisation through *real* leadership in the form of clear role modelling of values that would underpin future success. The culture had been characterised by hard work and very long working hours. He recognised that the future well-being of the company depended on working smarter, not harder. At least once a week, he would make a big thing of leaving the office early, saying he was going home to spend some quality time with his family.

- Finally, I witnessed a managing director of a professional services company bring about a sharp increase in performance in an organisation that was already performing well. The managing director thought that performance could actually be significantly better, and that its people were not stretching themselves so she had a choice to make. She could either play it safe and oversee the continued success of the organisation and enjoy her popularity when it came to bonus time, or she could challenge her people to stretch themselves and achieve their true potential. She chose the *real* leader option and started to communicate her thoughts around how she believed the future of the organisation was threatened by a complacency that was becoming ever more apparent. Her calls for everyone to raise the performance bar were met with derision among her people, but it was the foundation of the company's step change to the next performance level.

The differences between *real* and *safe* leaders are particularly evident and pronounced during tough and turbulent times for organisations. Remember, what lies at the core of the *safe* leader will mainly be about role security. This leader values the prestige, status, power, authority and the financial package that comes with leadership. There is a lot to lose for this leader, so much so that, particularly in tough times, his or her main focus will be staying out of the firing line and becoming even more risk-averse. To them, not taking risks means ensuring no mistakes. They withdraw into a safety zone; now is the time to avoid conflict and it becomes all too risky to challenge peers' or bosses' views. They spend less time coaching their people and more time telling their 'subordinates' what to do and how to do it. Careful in what they say, they sit tight in the hope that more favourable times are just around the corner. Their focus is on cutting costs and hitting short-term targets.

Contrast that with the approach of the *real* leader. Remember, such leaders are driven mainly by the challenge and opportunity to put themselves out there, make a difference and have a real impact. Tough times are their calling; they come to the fore and are even more highly visible. They focus on what they can control and make things happen. *Real* leaders make and stand by their decisions and 'tell it how it is'. They view tough economic climates as being when development is most needed; this is the time to nurture and retain talent in order to gain competitive advantage in the longer-term. Their skills are probably even more prominent as they strive to lead the organisation and support their people through turbulent, and sometimes catastrophic, circumstances. This is where their own personal resources are so important, to the extent that they are visible to their people. Their resilience, optimism balanced with realism, strength of character, vast experience, care and determination will be very evident but so, too, will be the fact that they are human beings like everyone else. They also have doubts and worries and there is no point hiding them. *Real* leaders are authentic and their impact in organisations is much more a function of *how they are* than *what they do*.

It is important to emphasise before moving on that I have thus far focused on the extremes of *real* and *safe* leadership in order to draw out key differences. Of course, the situation in organisations is much more complex than a simple delineation between the two. Since these leadership 'styles' are driven by core motives, leaders will have a propensity to be *real* or *safe*. However, leaders will move back and forth along the continuum when the situation demands it. There are times when risks and challenging those above are not in the best interests of the organisation. And, in what have been difficult economic times over several years, I am often asked, 'Surely what organisations need right now are *safe* leaders because they provide a *safe* pair of hands?' A *safe* pair of hands and a *safe* leader are not the same thing! *Safe* leadership is driven by the motives and intent of the leader; a *safe* pair of hands is underpinned by the ability and qualities of the leader. A leader who is seen as a safe pair of hands can still be a *real* leader, who is highly visible and focuses on the future and a plan for doing things differently and better.

I have also been asked how the *real/safe* distinction is different to the conventional leader/manager distinction, where the leader focuses on people and the future and the manager focuses on tasks and the current. At first sight, there are indeed some similarities. *Safe* leaders, like the conventional notion of 'the manager', work on tasks and immediate day-to-day issues; and *real* leaders, like the conventional notion of 'the leader', devote their time to people and creating a road map for the future. However, these similarities are based on how leaders spend their time and *what they do*. The *real/safe* distinction is founded on the motives that drive what they focus on and *how they are*. The examples of *real* and *safe* leaders described earlier in this section are underpinned not on what they did as such, but by their motives, values and mindsets – courage, conviction, care and putting the organisation's interests first, versus fear, avoidance and self-interest – that drove their behaviours. It is the motives, values, mindsets and intent that are the factors that determine how they are, moving far beyond the conventional leader/manager distinction. The *real/safe* distinction explains a wide range of leadership behaviours that the leader/manager distinction does not, such as why some leaders are reluctant to receive feedback whilst others are hungry for it, and why some leaders are reluctant and slow to address underperformance whilst others tackle it as soon as they are aware of it.

What impact do they have?

Top performance will not be delivered, at least at a sustainable level, in an organisation where *safe* leaders abound. As shown in Figure 4.2.2, they take the safer option and focus on the short-term – hitting the numbers. This is what leaders are generally incentivised on; it is how stakeholders measure their performance. It is also 'convenient' for *safe* leaders to focus on the short-term because they are dragged into the functional detail and simply do not have enough time to focus on the future – at least, that is what they claim! The impact, at its worst, is likely to be what was described in Part 3.3 as an 'urgent' environment characterised by:

- High pressure because the emphasis on short-term performance is combined with the lack of support and a vision
- Potential conflict among individuals and teams because of the short-term urgency to produce results
- People not feeling valued because they are unsure how the performance that is demanded of them contributes to the future of the organisation
- The short-term performance focus resulting in micromanagement
- 'Unhealthy competition' existing in the form of a lack of willingness to work effectively in teams because the 'big picture' is unclear, failing to share best practice and a focus on 'beating' your colleagues

• An 'avoidance' mentality existing because of the consequences of failing or making mistakes

Other likely consequences on the environment of *safe* leadership are that there will be a strong sense of politics and posturing; it may not be about how good people are but rather 'who they know'. People may feel there is a lot of whispering in corners and that a lot happens behind closed doors.

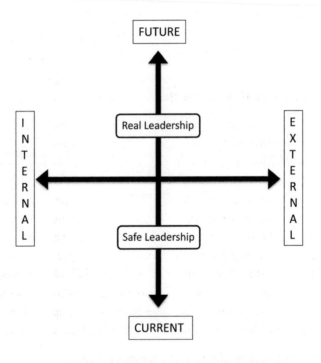

Figure 4.2.2 The strategic focus of *real* and *safe* leaders.

Real leaders, on the other hand, recognise that their responsibility is to focus more on the longer-term – 'innovation' and, in particular, 'well-being'. These are what the long-term health of the organisation is dependent upon. As I described in Part 3.1, getting the focus right in these areas means that the impact these *real* leaders have is that:

- People have a sense of relative freedom and discretion
- Responsible mistakes are allowed
- There is a high level of expectant energy
- There is a leading-edge mentality
- People feel valued, supported and listened to
- Commitment, loyalty and collaboration are high
- The retention rate of top performers is high

Nurturing *real* leadership

Real leaders hold the key to top performance and the future health of all organisations. Yet, too often, organisations and their leaders allow *safe* leaders to perpetuate the status quo and hinder progress and innovation. For example, as emphasised in Part 1.1, despite knowing better, organisations still make the mistake of promoting people to leadership positions based on criteria related much more to functional expertise than leadership capability. These people are rewarded for being good as a functional manager and the safer option when they find themselves with the difficult challenge of leading people is to bury themselves in micromanagement. Therefore, being a top performance leader means opting for a *real* approach, which requires a mindset and behaviours that include:

- Accepting accountability when things go wrong
- Having the confidence to let go
- Being willing to make mistakes
- Having the courage to make and own tough decisions
- Having the conviction to do the 'right thing'

- Focusing on creating a road map for the future
- Accepting the responsibility to drive change
- Being comfortable with the visibility of being a good role model
- Striving for continual personal growth and learning

This mindset and associated behaviours mean that such leaders must be able to:

- Remain in control when the pressure is at its most ferocious
- Build a resilient self-belief
- Maintain motivation when things are tough
- Stay focused on the things that matter
- Harness thoughts and feelings so they remain positive
- Turn threats into opportunities
- Bounce back from setbacks
- Learn from mistakes

These are not attributes that are easily learned in personal skills workshops but can be developed in the form of a know-how that drives key aspects of sustainable leadership, as will be clear in Part 4.4.

Nurturing *real* leadership involves developing and supporting *real* leaders whilst challenging *safe* leaders. *Real* leaders take on the task of challenging those who are stuck or choose to be at the *safe* end of the leadership continuum. However, challenging *safe* leaders can be difficult! They are likely to exhibit classic symptoms of either 'denial' ('Leave me alone to be the good leader I already am') or 'resistance' ('I'm far too busy to attend that leadership programme'). Ways in which *real* leaders can help their *safe* counterparts to become more *real* include:

- Getting them to create and communicate visions to their teams. This ensures they are proactive in focusing on the future and, by going public on it with their team, become visible and 'own' it

- Ensuring they receive impactful developmental feedback on a regular basis rather than once a year during performance reviews. *Safe* leaders, at the extreme, do not want feedback, or are quick to dismiss any they receive that they do not like. So finding a way of ensuring they do receive 360-degree feedback on their leadership that makes an impact should compel them to action
- Providing them with a challenging coach who has permission to push them outside the boundaries of their safety zone, encouraging risk-taking, making the tough decisions they have been avoiding and getting them to think beyond what they believe has worked in the past
- Helping them set goals that will drive their day-to-day leadership behaviours rather than the annual review goals that get lost and forgotten for twelve months. These should be in the form of process goals around 'how to be' as opposed to 'what to do' as a leader

Supporting *real* leaders brings a different type of challenge. Such leaders want to explore and experiment as part of their continuous growth. They are eager to be stretched and feel constantly at the cutting edge of leadership. Some of the ways of supporting *real* leaders include:

- Inviting them to lead workstreams that are focused on change initiatives
- Recognising these *real* leaders and endorsing their behaviours in public forums
- Finding ways of providing them with a voice in the organisation by facilitating access to the most senior leaders. They want to share their innovative views and ideas with their bosses; they are also keen to provide feedback on what is and what is not working
- *Real* leaders are hungry for feedback so ensuring that processes are in place outside the formal performance reviews is important

- Providing access to a coach who can help them with their feelings of loneliness and isolation – their high visibility means they will experience these feelings from time to time. The coach should also support their development of mental toughness to enable such leaders to thrive on the pressure
- Providing them with a mentor who they can bounce ideas off and who keeps them stimulated
- Giving them access to the latest thinking on leadership, perhaps in the form, for example, of sending them to thought leadership conferences and seminars, where they can feed off like-minded leaders from other organisations

Conclusion

Top performance leaders have at their core motives and values that drive their focus, behaviour and intent to be *real*. They are aware of their role modelling responsibility and nurture other leaders to assume the same mantle. Above all, top performance leaders are aware of the need to adapt and shape their approach to create the environment required to deliver the defined performance aspirations. Sometimes this means stretching themselves significantly, and this is where the support of their team and their ability to sustain themselves is important.

4.3 Team leadership

I have worked with too many teams to actually recall them all, but they have approached me with a huge variety of wants and needs, including:

- Newly formed teams who require some 'get to know each other' time

- Virtual teams who are searching for cohesion
- Dysfunctional teams who need to be functional
- Good teams, who want to make the transition to being great
- Working groups who need to be teams
- Siloed teams who want to be aligned with one voice

Sport has been an obvious area for organisations to begin their search for people like me to help them. One of the important learning points from sport relates to the countless examples of teams with reputably the best individual talent and ability which have fallen short of performance expectations. Top-performing teams, therefore, do not necessarily have the best individual talent and ability available, which means that other variables such as motivation, respect, responsibility and communication are of paramount importance.

I was put on the spot a couple of years ago by the CEO of a large global auction house, who asked me, 'In your experience of working with senior leadership teams, what is the most common cause of them not working effectively?' Now this may appear a fairly harmless question requiring an obvious answer, but I had never thought about teams in this specific context before. I began my answer by listing the things I have come across so many times in dysfunctional teams:

- Team members are good individually but a lack of synergy results in ill discipline
- The team is effective but not top-performing because lack of ambition leads to a 'doing enough' mentality
- Poor trust and respect issues cause a silo mentality
- Strong personality clashes underpin disruptive personal conflict
- Big egos drive an unhealthy competition
- An underlying fear among team members results in politeness, lack of openness and failure to address hard issues

- The team sees little value in actually working as a team and ends up operating as a working group
- Lack of vision for the team leads to short-termism and firefighting
- Entrenched opinions result in inflexibility
- The purpose of the team is unclear so that focus and cohesion is lacking
- Individuals just do not know how to work as a team

Having shared these, I eventually concluded the common denominator in all of the above is 'the leader'! It is the leader who allows these motives, mindsets and behaviours to germinate, infiltrate and eventually take over the workings of senior leadership teams. This can simply result from leaders devoting so much time to focusing on the wider organisation and the external marketplace that they lose sight of things right under their nose – including their own team. Their assumption that the team will 'look after itself' and just 'get on with things' means it can be mystifying and perplexing for such leaders to find themselves leading underperforming and/or dysfunctional teams.

There are, of course, other explanations but they all somehow find their way back to the leadership of the team. Leading a senior leadership team typically involves managing egos, strong opinions and personalities; these are bright people who may think they know best and probably believe they can do a better job than the leader. Leading these teams can be so hard that leaders may take the easy option of treating them as working groups rather than attempting to mould them as teams. Issues are easier left unaddressed because it consumes too much of the leader's time and emotional energy to 'fix' them.

Sometimes the leader is the very source of the dysfunctionality. A style of team leadership that is too strong will be overpowering and eventually result in a team of 'yes people' who look to the leader for direction and every decision. On the other hand, leaders who are weak will succumb to the loudest and most persistent voices. In some cases it is the leader who possesses the biggest ego. Driven by an underlying insecurity, the leader will want to have all the answers him/herself, stifling discussion and probably failing to delegate. And where a leader errs on the side of being *safe* rather than *real*, there is likely to be a political undercurrent in the team where fear and survival are the primary drivers.

Top performance team leadership

Top performance team leaders recognise that the support of those closest to them is critical to the achievement of their aspirations for the organisation. This support is also highlighted in Part 4.4 as an essential element of Sustainable Leadership. Top performance team leadership is about devoting time and energy to inspiring, uniting and aligning people with different skills, personalities, strengths and weaknesses to become a top performance team. Recognising and managing inevitable functional tensions requires transparency and sensitivity to ensure the various functional heads with their different priorities remain aligned and feel that fairness has prevailed. Leading these teams involves generating healthy competition in which team members feel challenged to 'up their game', while at the same time feeling supported by one another in order to all achieve more success and growth.

I have already pinpointed the key aspects of underperforming and/or dysfunctional teams I have come across and the role that leaders play in creating and perpetuating them. Fortunately, I have also had the pleasure of working with numerous top performance teams. Without exception, the leader has been instrumental in shaping an environment and climate in which people can join together and thrive. Below are the key things that leaders have worked hard to create and put in place across the top performance teams I have worked with:

- Aligned purpose and focus – providing cohesion and a clear collective agenda
- Challenge and support – boundaries are continually being stretched in the knowledge that help is available
- Impactful feedback – given and received in a way that things are not taken personally
- Transparency – hard issues are addressed openly
- Healthy competition – egos are 'left at the door'
- Collective belief – in the ability of the team to deliver the defined performance
- Resilience – the capacity to deal collectively with high expectations and demands, bounce back from setbacks and learn from mistakes
- Huge trust – team members do not have to be best friends but mutual trust is imperative
- Shared leadership – all team members assume responsibility and ownership of the team's impact
- Non-negotiables – there are a few things stipulated by the leader that are not open to debate

These conditions are not created without skilful leadership and patience. There are no shortcuts and it takes time to work through the phases of transition involved. The following section describes a framework for creating and leading top performance teams and the things that need to be in place during the various stages of transition.

Transitioning to a top performance team

Transitioning to a top performance team can be thought of in terms of a simple series of three phases shown in Figure 4.3.1:

'Create', 'Unite', 'Perform' (CUP). Whilst the CUP Model[21] is most easily applicable to newly formed teams who naturally start at the 'create' phase, it can also be applied to long-standing teams that are striving to be top-performing and who may need to revisit the 'create' phase to, quite literally, recreate themselves. For example, I described a team earlier in the book (Part 2.2) as 'tired high achievers all working at a furious pace to achieve the company's vision of being excellent'. This was an effective team that was unsure how to step up to the next level because of its uncertainty as to what 'excellent' actually meant. It was a clear example of an 'effective' team striving to make the transition to 'top-performing' but who needed to revisit what for them was the 'recreate' phase to make the key difference by redefining the vision.

Figure 4.3.1 describes a number of aspects of how teams transition through the various phases:

- **'Transition from'** identifies the beginning and end points of the transition in each phase
- **'Leader's checklist'** highlights the things that leaders need to ensure happen or are in place for the transition to be successful
- **'Leaders should expect'** identifies some of the typical emotions, mindsets and behaviours that are likely to be evident as progress is made through each phase
- **'Leaders should be wary of'** reflects some of the undesirable and unhelpful motives and behaviours among team members that might hinder progress through each phase

---

21 The research evidence underpinning the CUP Model and its constituent parts can be found in G. Jones. 'Performance excellence: A personal perspective on the link between sport and business'. *Journal of Applied Sport Psychology*, 2002, 268–281.

	CREATE → (Teambuilding)	UNITE → (Teamworking)	PERFORM (Impact)
Transition from:	Defining & Planning → Commitment Performance	Exploration → Cohesion	Effective →Top Performing
Leader's checklist:	**Clarity** • Purpose • Vision/performance aspirations • Goals, priorities and time frames • Roles, responsibilities and boundaries **Awareness** • Know each other • Non-negotiables • Performance environment **Agreement** • Values • Behaviours • Ways of working **Buy-in** • Collective belief in the team's potential • Declared actions • Team charter	**Execution** • Role conformity • Mutual ownership and accountability • Adherence to agreed values and behaviours • Meeting agendas aligned with team purpose **Stretch** • Feedback provided • Challenge • Renewed action **Engagement** • Full participation • Buy-in to consensus • Open communication • Members feel valued	**Trust** • Shared leadership • Shared mental model • Welcomed challenge • Feedback invited • Responsible risk-taking **Care** • Commitment to others' development • Care for each other • Supportive environment **Resilience** • Flexibility & adaptability • Learn from setbacks • 'Have one another's backs' • 'One voice' • Celebration of successes **Excellence** • Exceeding goals and expectations • Innovation
Leaders should expect:	• Politeness • Enthusiasm • Apprehension • Uncertainty	• Togetherness • Mutual support • Individual expression • Peer-to-peer challenge	• 'Edge' • Transparency • Difficult questions • Healthy competition • Succession-planning
Leaders should be wary of:	• 'Top dogs' • 'Nodding dogs' • 'Charlatans' • 'Mercenaries' • 'Avoiders'	• 'Paralysers' • 'Elephants' • 'Hermits' • 'Renegades' • 'Donkeys'	• 'Prima donnas' • 'Heroes' • 'Villains' • 'Swashbucklers' • 'Stragglers'

Figure 4.3.1 The CUP Model.

Create

The CUP Model begins with the premise that the key to team building is to 'create' a positive psychological environment that facilitates the transition from 'defining and planning performance' to 'commitment'. 'Defining and planning performance' involves being clear about what the team is trying to achieve and how and when it will get there. Devoting quality time to discussing and agreeing the 'why', 'what', 'who' and 'when' is an imperative before moving on to spending further quality time exploring and agreeing the 'how'. 'Commitment' represents the buy-in to the actioned output agreed during this phase. Leaders can only be sure that the team is actually committed to the output of these discussions and activities when they have 'signed up' to actions and behaviours.

This phase can be equally applicable for long-standing teams as it is for newly formed ones. The source of dysfunctional teams which operate in transactional silos driven by self-interest, for example, can often be traced back to uncertainty regarding the team's purpose and individual roles, as well as weak personal connections because they have not spent time getting to know each other as more than just colleagues. Indeed, I never fail to be astonished by the number of teams I come across who are either unsure of or cannot agree on their purpose. This is why so many teams spend too much time discussing topics that should be dealt with elsewhere; their default is to get into detail and usually the operational matters that others outside the team are being tasked and paid to do.

Devoting quality time to achieving *clarity* around the purpose of any team must occur before performance aspirations which are compelling for all team members, commonly in the form of a vision, can be defined. This is where the team requires a firm steer from the leader because it is he or she who will have had more exposure to the broader context. However, it is critical that the purpose and vision has total buy-in from the whole team, so this steer must be carefully balanced by a sensitivity that allows others to have their say and feel that they are being listened to. The team vision must, of course, be aligned with the organisational vision and include clear time frames and goals and priorities in order to monitor progress and keep the team on track. All team members want to see how their contributions fit into achieving the vision so clear roles and responsibilities are also essential. Clarifying boundaries will help to minimise duplication of effort and focus, as well as any frustration caused by 'stepping on toes'.

Developing *awareness* among the team also requires quality time. Getting to understand and respect the differences that exist within the team will help it gel more quickly. Different skills, experiences, preferences, personalities, priorities and personal circumstances bring a variety of strengths that may, at best, go unnoticed and untapped until opportunities are provided for this information to be disclosed. At worst, these differences may cause friction and conflict that undermine the team's functioning. Leaders are commonly advised to 'get to know their people' but top performance team leadership is also about allowing their people to get to know *them*. Disclosing a couple of vulnerabilities, as simple as 'I don't have all the answers,' for example, can go a long way towards forging an emotional connection between the leader and the team. The team leader should be clear about his or her non-negotiables and also make them clear to the team. These should be just two or three things that s/he *really* values and believes are critical to the team's success, meaning the leader is able to empower the team on the grounds that everything else is negotiable. Also, a shared awareness and understanding of the obstacles and constraints that exist in the performance environment, as well as the potential supports, is essential to enabling the team to work *with* rather than being victims of the environment to deliver success.

Reaching *agreement* on fundamental aspects of how the team will work together is made easier by the clarity and awareness achieved in the areas described above. Agreeing the values that the team are not willing to compromise on will drive behavioural norms and expectations of each other. I have lost count of the times I have heard 'integrity' and 'openness' being espoused across all nature of teams, but values such as these are only meaningful when explicit behaviours are attached to them. What do they *really* mean in the day-to-day operation of the team? Ways of working should be driven by these values and behaviours as the team agrees on things like methods and boundaries of communication and frequency of team meetings.

Of course, the clarity, awareness and agreement are only as good as the subsequent *buy-in*. Underpinning buy-in is a collective belief in the team's potential and ability to deliver the performance aspirations, and the leader must challenge anyone whose belief s/he feels might be wavering. Declared actions at an individual level represent a powerful means of assessing and monitoring commitment and should be continually revisited and updated. A team charter can also be helpful so long as it, too, is subject to continual reinforcement and updating. I have found team charters to be particularly impactful when shared with direct reports and their respective teams. For example, I once worked with a management board in an industrial services organisation who shared their charter in this way, asking the people reporting into them to hold them accountable to it. Their direct reports found it so impactful that they used the same charter with their own teams.

Typical of the transition during this phase from 'defining and planning performance' to 'commitment' is a *politeness* among the team when they are together. My experience informs me that there are lots of polite teams across all types of organisations and performance domains. Such teams are characterised by an overdone level of care to not upset or tread on the toes of colleagues, which drives a level of sensitivity that results in superficial discussions and debates where strong views and opinions are held back. This politeness combined with an *enthusiasm* resulting from new challenges and circumstances makes for a 'nice' environment in the earliest stages of transition. It may be too early for team members to overtly express their *apprehension* and *uncertainty* and a key skill of the leader is to create the conditions where individuals can begin to disclose these feelings. This is the phase for laying the foundations of trusting relationships.

Unfortunately, no matter how smoothly the team transitions through the 'create' phase, potential undesirable and unhelpful distractions constantly lurk around the corner. Some of the more obvious ones requiring leaders' vigilance are:

- 'Top dogs' – people whose 'superiority complex' gets the better of them and who value their own expertise, ability and views above those of their colleagues
- 'Nodding dogs' – people who say 'yes' to everything but have no intention of adhering
- 'Charlatans' – people who claim to be what they are not and to be able to do what they cannot
- 'Mercenaries' – people who continually posture and position themselves to ensure their self-interest comes before the best interests of the team
- 'Avoiders' – people who fail to commit to anything that has a risk associated with it

Unite

The next phase in the CUP Model, 'unite', involves focusing on teamworking as the team transitions from 'exploration' to 'cohesion'. 'Exploration' is where the team tries and tests the ways of working agreed in the previous phase and makes modifications and sometimes significant changes. 'Cohesion' is where the team comes together as a single unit moving in the same direction. Again, this phase can be equally applicable for long-standing teams as it is for newly formed ones. Teams that are effective but are struggling to become top-performing may need to revisit the fundamentals of being cohesive in the form, perhaps, of reminding themselves of the bigger picture or reviewing processes to ensure full participation in key decision-making.

The day-to-day operation of the team is fundamentally about the *execution* of the agreements and commitments reached in the previous phase. Conforming to defined roles brings about a certainty and stability which allows the team to try and test the ways of working they discussed at length earlier. Mutual ownership and accountability means that individual team members can focus on their priorities with the confidence that others are also 'doing their bit'. Adherence to agreed values and behaviours is fundamental in the successful move from exploration to cohesion. Positive peer pressure is important in this context since it should be all team members' responsibility, and not just that of the leader, to ensure that agreements made during the 'create' or teambuilding phase are adhered to. Meetings are an inevitable and unavoidable aspect of teamwork and it is incumbent on the leader to ensure that items do not creep on to the agenda that are not aligned with the team's purpose.

Stretch is an essential part of the team's journey to becoming top-performing, and the leader must create conditions where the team feels willing and able to give one another feedback which is best intentioned in the context of the team's growth. This almost always feels awkward to both giver and receiver during this phase of the team's development, as is the challenge that is also required if the team are to move forward. Both feedback and challenge must result in commitment to renewed action. Evidence of this renewed action, or lack of it, is a rich source of information to the leader regarding team members' potential contributions to becoming a top performance team.

Engagement is where there is full participation in things like decision-making and meetings because team members want to participate rather than feel obliged to. It is not always possible to reach agreement and engagement means a buy-in to consensus followed by communication and behaviours that reinforce it. Open communication is often a positive sign of engagement and it also reflects that individuals feel valued and that they are listened to.

Moving from 'exploration' to 'cohesion' during this phase will be accompanied by an increasing sense of *togetherness*, where people build pride and a loyalty to the team. Commitment to actions resulting from feedback and challenge will ensure *mutual support* as team members strive to collaborate and add value. *Individual expression* of views and opinions should be expected and welcomed as the team debates how to optimise their teamworking. *Challenge* may be confined to the *peer-to-peer* level since it may be too early to challenge the leader, at least in a public forum. The leader should therefore operate an 'open door' policy whereby individuals can express their concerns and ask questions related to the leadership of the team.

As the team explores ways of working in the quest for cohesion, there will inevitably be things that might get in the way of progress. Some of the more common ones include:

- 'Paralysers' – people who fail to take action because of their fear of failure, and also those who are comfortable and wish to keep things as they are rather than be agents of change
- 'Elephants' – the unspoken yet all-consuming things that act as blockers to effective teamworking

- 'Hermits' – people who want to do things on their own, thus threatening cohesion and creating silos
- 'Renegades' – dissidents or mutineers who either loudly disagree or quietly operate in the background to influence opinion and build barriers to the team's cohesion
- 'Donkeys' – people who are unable to say 'no' and are the saviours of the shirkers who pass on their workload to willing subservients

Perform

Of course, the team will have been performing since its inception but this phase focuses explicitly on its impact and stepping up performance levels in order to transcend from being 'effective' to 'top-performing'. There are four essentials that leaders must ensure happen or are in place for the team to become top-performing: trust, care, resilience and excellence.

Trust is where team members start to share the leadership of how the team functions. This does not, of course, mean that *the* leader absolves responsibility but requires him or her to have the confidence to take a step backwards and let others take ownership of initiatives and actions. A shared mental model whereby everyone in the team has the same mental representation of what is demanded and how to deliver it will enhance this process. This, in turn, will drive a challenge among the team that is best intentioned and welcomed. The leader should role model and invite developmental feedback aimed at moving the team forward from being 'effective' to 'top-performing'. Strong trust in the team encourages responsible risk-taking, which is essential to guaranteeing continual growth and a feeling of being at the edge.

The journey to top performance will require *care* for one another. Top performance teams have people who are committed to their personal development as well as being committed to supporting the personal development of their colleagues. Their care for one another's well-being means that they make time for one another to offer and provide support on both work-related and personal challenges. This engenders a supportive environment where people feel able to disclose their challenges, vulnerabilities and development areas and ask for help. Again, the leader's role modelling is key to creating a caring environment where people know that support is close at hand.

Top-performing teams operate in an environment where the demands can change constantly and where *resilience* in the form of flexibility and adaptability are required to accommodate and respond rapidly and appropriately to them. Things will not always go to plan and the leader must ensure that every setback is a source of learning. 'Having one another's backs' is a phrase commonly heard in top performance teams and is especially important during and after those setbacks. 'One voice' is another phrase used commonly and reflects the commitment to delivering agreed and consistent messages to interested parties outside the team. An important essential in building the resilience to move from 'effective' to 'top-performing' is to celebrate the successes of the team. Leaders should ensure that time is set aside for success to not only be enjoyed but also to extract key learning.

The obvious difference between 'effective' and 'top-performing' teams is the consistent delivery of *excellence*. Effective teams will deliver what they are asked and expected to deliver. Top-performing teams consistently exceed externally focused goals, as well as the stretching internally focused goals they have set for themselves. Innovation is also critical in top performance teams, who constantly push boundaries to keep performance levels on an upward gradient.

Being a top performance team brings with it an *'edge'* to the team's dynamics and dialogue; feedback is direct, plentiful and impactful in a way that is not taken personally because both giver and receiver only engage in it believing that it will enhance performance in some way. *Transparency* is paramount as the leader opens him or herself up to expect and welcome challenge and *difficult questions* because s/he also knows that it is given only with the best intentions in mind. Ideas are abundant and received with an openness that encourages even more. At some point, the leader will need to impose his or her own 'edge' to ensure the team moves from discussion and debate to action. Only under these conditions can *healthy competition* prevail and help to inspire and push team members to even higher levels of performance. Finally, top performance teams know they can never stand still: continual change is necessary if complacency, stagnation and overfamiliarisation are to be kept at arm's length. This means that the composition of the team will regularly be under review as part of a *succession-planning* process that keeps the team moving onwards and upwards.

The 'edge' associated with top performance teams does have potential risks that require leaders' close vigilance. Some of the more common ones include:

- 'Prima donnas' – people who are difficult to lead because their big but often fragile egos mean that they are 'high maintenance' and likely to blame others for their mistakes
- 'Heroes' – people who constantly put themselves on the line and are at serious risk of burnout
- 'Villains' – people who try to outdo their colleagues sometimes by foul means, such as putting down others' achievements and generally causing unhealthy competition
- 'Swashbucklers' – people who get carried away with success and believe they are invincible, leading them to enter into irresponsible risks
- 'Stragglers' – team members who are struggling to keep up with the fast pace and demands but they are unwilling to ask for help.

Conclusion

Top performance leaders know that they cannot deliver on their own and that they need the support of those closest to them if their leadership is to be *real* and remain sustainable. Creating a top performance team clearly takes time, effort and a knowledge of how to do so. The CUP Model represents an easy-to-follow guide which can also be used as a diagnostic to assess where teams are in the process, as well as what aspects might need to be revisited. Getting things right in the 'create'phase, or what might be the 'recreate' phase for some teams, is fundamental to establishing the foundation and building blocks from which the team can grow. I have already described how, in my experience, teams struggle to evolve and unite because the purpose, the very reason for their existence, is unclear. Top performance team leaders have crystal-clear clarity and ensure that everything the team does and focuses on is in complete alignment.

Top performance team leaders also have confidence in their people, as well as in themselves, to let go. This is reflected in a shared leadership in which everyone contributes and assumes ownership of the team's functioning and output. Role modelling the 'edge' they expect from their team is something these leaders are good at, ensuring that they act decisively and quickly when circumstances demand it. One of the basic assumptions of the CUP Model is that the ability and/or mindset of the team members is appropriate to the team's needs. This is not always the case, of course, and there are numerous potential distractions and disruptions that require the leader's close vigilance. Sometimes, these are not 'fixable' and top performance leaders are strong in making the necessary personnel changes. They are quick to address these issues because they apply their own 'edge' in the best interests of the team, and they also know that their credibility will be questioned if they do not.

4.4 Sustainable leadership

I am privileged to have had some amazing experiences in my work with top performers and leaders in several performance domains. My curiosity and intrigue with exactly what sets these people aside from those who do not make it to the top led to devoting an academic career to the scientific study of it. More recently, I have become especially interested in what enables them to stay at the top when they get there. This is particularly important for top performance leaders because their motive to be *real* rather than *safe* brings with it the visibility and exposure that can drain and eventually overwhelm those who are unprepared or ill-equipped for it. There are a growing number of unfortunate stories that bear ample witness to this, where leaders have stepped down or taken a leave of absence due to reported fatigue, exhaustion and stress.

Sustainability and longevity as a leader has never been more in jeopardy as leaders are faced with increasing scrutiny of their day-to-day performance. Countless KPIs, performance reviews, competency ratings and 360-degree feedback are just a few of the metrics that expose individual leadership performance at an unprecedented level. This is exacerbated by an ever-demanding world in which delivering the numbers alone is no longer sufficient to satisfy key stakeholders; the results delivered must be both socially responsible and sustainable. Herein lies the greatest challenge facing organisations and the leaders and teams working within them. Delivering a one-off top performance is comparatively easy – delivering it time and again is a very different proposition!

So what is it that enables leaders to deliver success time and again, rather than succumbing to their *real* leadership demands of being highly visible, scrutinised and accountable? Having observed top performers and leaders at very close quarters in a variety of arenas over several years, I have come to realise that they possess what I believe to be a form of wisdom or know-how. It is very evident among the world's best athletes and I have also witnessed it among the best leaders and performers in other performance settings.

The scientist's mindset that continues to drive my curiosity means that I do not expect you to accept a treatise based on experience alone. The detail of the know-how underpinning sustainable leadership originates from a scientific study I conducted of top performers and leaders from the worlds of business, sports, military, performing arts and medicine[22]. The study involved in-depth interviews with an amazing group of twelve men and women who have demonstrated sustained success in a single field over a prolonged period or have been successful in more than one field. Specifically, five of those interviewed had achieved the highest levels of performance over a minimum period of ten years in their chosen field. They comprised the most senior leader in an elite fighting force, an entrepreneur renowned for being innovative and successful in the financial sector, a performing artist (ballet dancer) who had danced at the highest levels and two chief executive officers, one of whom led a large global charity and the other in the postal service industry. The remaining seven people had been successful in more than one performance domain. Three of them were Olympic gold medal winners (Rowing and Track and Field) before being successful in the world of professional services. Two others had achieved success in American football (one a Super Bowl winner and the other an All-American college player) before moving on to careers that ultimately resulted in achieving senior leadership status in large global commercial organisations. The All-American college player also had a successful career in the military before moving into the commercial world. Another interviewee had

22 G. Jones. 'The role of Superior Performance Intelligence in sustained success'. In S. Murphy (Ed.), *Oxford Handbook Of Sport and Performance Psychology*. Oxford: Oxford University Press, 2012.

won an Olympic gold medal (Modern Pentathlon) before pursuing a successful career as a medical doctor. The final person in the 'successful across more than one domain' category was the head of a heart surgery team in a leading hospital before becoming a senior leader in a large pharmaceutical company.

The study revealed that sustainable leadership may be thought of as comprising the three core know-hows[23] shown in Figure 4.4.1.

- 'Knowing how to self-actualise' comprises three dimensions that reflect a self-knowledge and ability to self-regulate in order to realise one's capability and potential:
  - self-knowledge
  - growth
  - resilience
- 'Knowing how to work *with* the environment' comprises three dimensions that involve knowing how to shape and use the performance environment to advantage:
  - awareness
  - shaping
  - staying in tune
- 'Knowing how to deliver top performance' comprises three dimensions around the process of performing to high levels on a consistent basis:
  - preparation
  - delivery
  - evaluation

A gap or weakness in any of the know-hows will jeopardise longevity at the top. For example, the CEO of a company acquired by a much larger organisation had consistently hit the numbers and

---

23 Some of the know-how labels have been slightly modified to better fit with leadership rather than the wider performance arena.

so was good at 'knowing how to deliver top performance'. And he had risen quickly through the organisation, demonstrating strength in 'knowing how to self-actualise'. However, he was poor at 'knowing how to work *with* the environment'; his suspicions about the acquiring company's plans led to constant confrontation and working *against* the 'new environment' rather than *with* it. He role-modelled a 'victim mentality' that soured relations between his own people and the acquiring company. This gap in his sustainable leadership know-how had serious consequences: he was sacked!

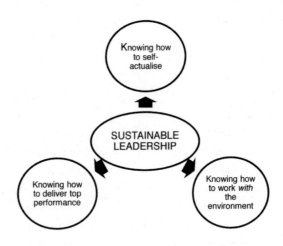

Figure 4.4.1 Sustainable leadership.

An example of a gap in a different area, 'knowing how to self-actualise', is the female country head of a pharmaceutical organisation whose prowess at 'knowing how to work *with* the environment' was evidenced by her creation of open and transparent communication processes among the senior leaders. The detailed plans and 'what if?' scenarios she had set in place for every KPI showed a real strength in 'knowing how to deliver top performance'.

However, she was seriously lacking when it came to 'knowing how to self-actualise'. She believed that she had been lucky to get to her current position and was 'waiting to be found out', which meant that her consensus-driven approach was driven by a fear of her people disagreeing with and challenging her. Also, she lacked a personal vision and was unsure of what she wanted her future career to look like. The consequence was that she was not the visible leader the business needed and was eventually sidelined to an operational role.

A gap in 'knowing how to deliver top performance' also threatens leadership longevity. The male divisional head of a well-known brand I worked with was clearly strong at 'knowing how to work *with* the environment' because he was popular with his people and had very good working relations with them. He had a high level of self-awareness regarding 'knowing how to self-actualise', and had worked hard on areas requiring personal development. Sadly, his gap in 'knowing how to deliver top performance' became his downfall; his failure to look ahead and plan for every scenario resulted in him getting surprised and derailed when things went wrong, and it also meant he failed to see opportunities when they arose. Fundamentally, he was unclear about what success looked like, and the consequence was that he was overlooked for promotion on a couple of occasions and left the organisation.

The following sections describe the detail underpinning each of the know-hows. They include quotes (*in italics*) taken directly from the interview transcripts emanating from the study described earlier in order to provide a richness and in-depth understanding of what constitutes the different know-hows.

Knowing how to self-actualise

I described in Part 3.4 how top performance leaders create the conditions and satisfy needs that enable the self-actualisation of their people. One of the foundations of sustainable leadership is their *own* self-actualisation: people who reach leadership positions in organisations are already high achievers and have gone a long way in realising their potential, but sustainable leadership is about *maximising* one's potential through 'self-knowledge', 'growth' and 'resilience'. These dimensions and the specific areas of know-how underpinning each are shown in Figure 4.4.2.

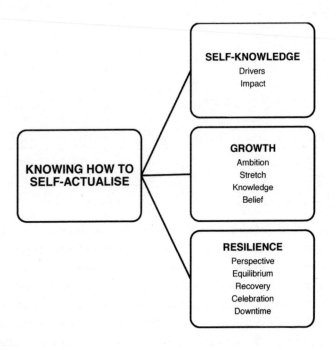

Figure 4.4.2 Knowing how to self-actualise.

Self-knowledge. This self-knowledge involves a distinction between *who* and *how* they are as leaders based on their internal drivers and external impact respectively:

- **Drivers:** Knowing *who* they are as a leader
  - *'Knowing who I am, I think, is around value sets'*
  - *'It's about understanding who you are and understanding what is important to you and not compromising on the things that are important'*
  - *'Knowing deeply who you are and sticking with that and being comfortable with that'*

- **Impact:** Knowing *how* they are as a leader
  - *'Knowing how you are is more about knowing yourself in a social context … I've always been very aware of the impact I have on other people'*
  - *'It helps me to understand how I think, behave and manage and it enables me to think about how other people might be thinking about how I'm behaving and managing'*
  - *'I'm not that different at work than I am at home and I don't have a strain about putting on a guise … it can be confusing to the boys because I'm a General and I often don't behave quite like one … I behave like a General when I know I need to'*

This self-knowledge about *who* they are as leaders enables an awareness of what is most important to them and what drives them, and feeling comfortable with that. Self-knowledge about *how* they are is more akin to emotional intelligence in the form of how their drivers manifest in their behaviours and what might need modifying to better suit the needs of the environment and those around them. Both aspects of 'self-knowledge' are fundamental to understanding what they are capable of and the implications for stretching themselves.

Growth. This dimension reflects a continual striving for self-improvement as a leader and comprises four specific areas of know-how:

- **Ambition:** Having a personal vision
  - *'I had an epiphany when I was about twenty that there was injustice in the world and my vision was to dedicate my life to doing something about injustice, whatever form that takes, and my personal vision has been to make a difference ... and then I had a moment in my late twenties when I said I'm pretty good at leading people and I want to inspire and motivate people and I want to lead an organisation, lead on an issue, and that was when I wanted to be a CEO of an organisation dedicated to fighting injustice'*
  - *'A lack of vision hurts ... you can't plan if you don't have a vision ... lots of people don't have an idea of what they're trying to do and so have no chance of getting there'*

- **Stretch:** Striving to be the best they can
  - *'If you don't have that (desire) then you're not going to be the best you can'*
  - *'Even now, I want to be the best doctor that I can be ... I want to know that I'm doing the right thing for my patients'*

- **Knowledge:** Being a sponge for learning
  - *'Continuous learning ... never stop, even if you don't have a goal to aim for'*
  - *'I read about new things that will give me new knowledge and continuously reinforce my excitement about the job'*
  - *'I once read a quote that "feedback is the breakfast of champions" and I fully believe that ... one of the biggest pitfalls I see in senior leaders is that they become incapable of taking constructive criticism ... they've created these barriers to negative feedback and they have this open door to positive feedback so that they end up losing touch with reality ... to me, feedback keeps you in touch with reality and the higher you go in an organisation, the more you have to seek feedback because it won't be given to you voluntarily'*
  - *'People get so scared that they're not prepared to try new things ...*

you know the more senior they become, the more cautious and guarded they become because they're always worried about being seen to be foolish … I always ask questions about the things I don't understand, and very often lots of people don't understand as well and they go, "Thank goodness the General doesn't understand"'

- **Belief:** Having a fundamental self-belief
  - *'Once you're at the top, it's having the belief and confidence that you can deliver repeatable top performance, a belief that enables you to keep stretching yourself'*
  - *'A confidence to be relaxed in your own skin'*
  - *'"Knowing" you can win versus "hoping" you can win'*

Leaders' 'growth' begins with having a personal vision that provides them with long-term aspirations that keep them moving in the right direction. Their daily drive is underpinned simply by wanting to be the best they can in everything they do. At the core of stretching oneself is a desire and commitment to continuous learning via sources of new knowledge, trying new ways of doing things, and seeking and acting on feedback. Their willingness to admit and accept that they do not have all the answers accompanied by an openness to new and different ideas is an outward sign of their fundamental belief in themselves.

Resilience. Sustainability is about having a resilience that helps leaders deal positively with the challenges of being a top performance leader. At the core of resilience are:

- **Perspective:** Keeping the bigger picture in mind
  - *'Whether you're in sport or in a business, you're going to have high highs and low lows and it's important to keep perspective of the big picture … there are going to be highs and there are going to be lows and that's what makes you stronger over time … don't let the lows get you down too much, don't let the highs make you too cocky'*

- o *'That's one of the reasons I travel ... I want to get out and remind ourselves what the bigger picture is and why you sit in this glass office and do what you do'*
- o *'I keep coming back to the bigger picture about who I am in terms of values and balance and that kind of thing and it helps get me back on track when I'm veering off'*

- **Equilibrium:** Achieving a good life balance
  - o *'I'm a better doctor for having the time out with my children ... if I was consulting full-time I just couldn't do that, I think my patients benefit because I get a better balance in terms of life'*
  - o *'It's having ways of contextualising what you do and not being so busy making a living that you've failed to make a life ... you can quite easily become completely absorbed ... when you have a responsibility for people, it's an unlimited liability'*
  - o *'I failed at this during my twenties and thirties ... I was really driven and was a workaholic ... it's much better now and there's two reasons ... one is a self-awareness ... I realised that I was on a gerbil's wheel and that I needed to find something much more internal to be happy with my reason to be and that I didn't have to just define myself by myself and by my work ... I found a way to define myself with work as part of that but not the sum of it ... and the other one is now I have a family ... having a family is something that pulls you out of work ... I can't wait to get home to see my kids now'*

- **Recovery:** Bouncing back from failures and setbacks
  - o *'You have to be prepared to lose, you have to be prepared to tough it out when things are down'*
  - o *'I think part of the willingness or the ability to be flexible is also recognition that you don't have enough wisdom and it's alright to fail ... it's alright to fail and to be seen to fail, people want to be led by human beings'*

- o *'I sometimes think I personalise it too much but I also think I'm able to move on pretty quickly ... I absorb it and then I get rid of it pretty quickly'*

- **Celebration:** Enjoying successes
  - o *'When we won in Bled, the opposition was not too strong, but I got the crew together and said, "We've got to enjoy when we win races, no matter who we've just beaten" ... an important part of my awareness over the years is that I should recognise and celebrate and enjoy success'*
  - o *'When we have a huge win here I celebrate big time with people on a Friday evening, but Monday morning I'm thinking, "Back at it" ... there are things and moments where I want to share in that glory but it's crucial to know when to refocus on the challenges ahead'*

- **Downtime:** Switching off
  - o *'It would be so intense you'd wear yourself into a frazzle ... there's a time when you need to rest and to refresh ... there's a time when there's just pure performance and emotion and there's a time to back off and let things settle and reflect'*
  - o *'Really addressing the "switch-off" time and having other things to do which still allow effective recovery but that allows the brain to stop thinking about that last session ... I go off and do something that I like to do but doesn't require much effort'*

Resilience in top performance leaders is very much about knowing how to achieve a personal equilibrium that enables them to deal effectively with the demands, pressures and potential distractions inherent in the process of delivering top performance on a consistent basis. There are inevitable highs and lows to deal with and keeping the bigger picture in mind helps provide perspective and meaning. Achieving a good life balance means that the time spent with colleagues or loved ones can be of a higher quality, whilst switching off provides a downtime for re-energising that is crucial for all top performance leaders' sustainability. Sustainable leadership involves recognising energy is a vital resource in limited supply and so must be used and allocated carefully. The acceptance that it is OK to fail can be hard to achieve but bouncing back and learning from it is a critical part of sustainable leadership. Finally, it is easy to move on too quickly after successes before they have been celebrated; top performance leaders recognise and enjoy success, but they also know when to stop celebrating and to move on to the next challenge before they become distracted by it.

Knowing how to work *with* the environment

This sustainable leadership know-how comprises three dimensions – 'awareness', 'shaping' and 'staying in tune' – that relate to leaders' ability to use the performance environment to their advantage and work *with* it rather than *against* it. The specific areas of know-how underpinning this dimension are shown in Figure 4.4.3.

Awareness. This dimension involves a detailed awareness of the performance environment and, specifically, distinguishing between knowledge and information about *controllable* and *uncontrollable* aspects of the performance environment:

- **Controllables:** Knowing the controllable environment
  - *'You can sometimes feel isolated and removed as a leader … I ask a lot of questions … I want to know what's going on, to take the pulse of the organisation and morale, purpose, etc. to see how and where I can help'*
  - *'I'm in a very busy GP practice … you know you're going to be under pressure, running late, receptionists hassling you for this and that … it's about knowing that that is the situation … you have to find your own ways of getting things done, prioritising things, time management, delegation'*

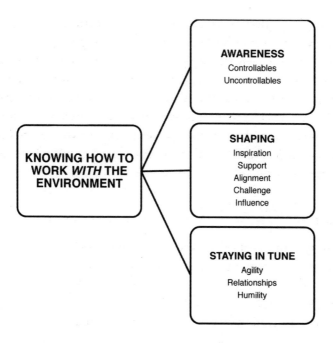

Figure 4.4.3 Knowing how to work *with* the environment.

- **Uncontrollables:** Knowing the uncontrollable environment
  - *'In (American) football, knowing the competition, knowing the game, even the stadium and where you're playing, whether it's hostile or not … those things were all very important … in business, obviously you've got to know your market, your customers, your competitors, the environmental regulations and governmental constraints, knowing the rules which you've got to play by and how the game's going to be played is absolutely critical to setting strategy and being successful'*
  - *'Know everything about what's out there and what you're up against … don't get surprised … don't lose sleep over it but use that knowledge when the time comes'*

This know-how focuses on understanding the reality of the environment so that leaders know the important things that are going on around them and what is in their control. However, it is not as simple as merely following the classic soundbite 'focus on controlling the controllables', since this carries with it the danger of being surprised by the uncontrollables that leaders have been encouraged *not* to focus on. Spending time identifying what is uncontrollable and understanding the impact those factors will have is vital. It is important to acknowledge them before putting these uncontrollables to one side whilst the focus turns to the things that *are* in leaders' control.

Shaping. This dimension covers the ability to create and shape the performance environment that will deliver sustained success and comprises:

- **Inspiration:** Defining and communicating the vision and goals
    - *'An ability to see around corners and what can be rather than what is'*
    - *'I've always worked hard at defining and communicating a vision that people buy into and creating a culture and belief that you can win, will win and here's why, how and when … once you create that, people not only buy into it, they take the extra steps to get the skill sets, the mental toughness to be successful, and that organisation can go anywhere because it has that capability of truly rising above any competition'*
    - *'Plan for the end result and work backwards … it won't happen just through raw talent … you have to have those stepwise goals to be able to get there'*

- **Support:** Surrounding oneself with the right people
    - *'Have players that can be successful in different types of situations … a diversified team'*

- o *'I was truly blessed with having several great people who coached me and their belief in me was huge'*
- o *'It's critically important to have trusted advisors and people you can go to when times are tough'*
- o *'You want to surround yourself with people who have the know-how, knowing you have access to the best advice, and apply it'*

- **Alignment:** Fostering collaboration
  - o *'If the desire to win is not in alignment against a common vision, a personal win will create ill-will or harm the overall team'*
  - o *'If you're the CEO you have to be aligned with the shareholders' goals, the customers' goals, the employees' goals and the community goals and have to get everybody working towards those goals'*
  - o *'Coming out of the NFL into the business world was one of the things that I had to truly learn to balance ... in pro football, unlike business, every year your employer brought in forty-five additional guys to come take your job so part of your focus had to be against your internal competition and until you were designated as a team you were trying to protect your role ... it was great for competition but in business that level of intensity can be detrimental to an organisation and to an individual ... when you start seeing your workmates as your competition it creates an unhealthy atmosphere ... so I had to learn to deal with that intellectually ... I had to learn to channel against the external competition and not internal competition'*

- **Challenge:** Challenging orthodoxy
  - o *'If you always do what you've always done, then you'll always get what you've always got ... a head hunter once wrote that I had a healthy sense of frustration ... you don't have to accept stuff and you should always push back on things you think aren't right'*
  - o *'We all get into ruts and if you want to truly outperform what everybody else is doing then you have to do something different and*

that means stretching out beyond what's normal … if you don't do that, you're not going to be the best'

- **Influence:** Using one's emotional intelligence to:
  - *'Read emotion in my colleagues'*
  - *'Know what's going on around me, what's going on for the people around me so that we're in sync with one another'*
  - *'Get the environment to adapt to me'*
  - *'Get the most out of the people around me'*
  - *'Influence people to do things they sometimes don't want to do or are very difficult to do, but doing it in a way that makes them want to do it'*

Shaping the environment in the context of sustainable leadership requires leaders to define and communicate a vision that is exciting and that people believe in. People want to be part of success and defining the end point can help them feel good about the journey and work extra-hard to get there. Underpinning the vision is a series of clearly defined goals mapping out how it will be achieved. Having the right people around them, who are versatile, good at what they do, resilient, trustworthy, team players and who constantly strive to find new and better ways of delivering success, is a must for top performance leadership to be sustainable. These people provide a constructive and best-intentioned upward challenge that keeps leaders on their toes and continually moving forward.

Staying in tune. The final dimension of the 'working *with* your environment' know-how relates to leaders' day-to-day interaction with the performance environment and comprises:

- **Agility:** Being agile
  - *'Being agile is critical but a challenge in a business where you've got governance, processes etc. as a really big deal, but you have to be,*

otherwise you get caught up in it and don't move the business on'
- o *'Dealing with a whole range of issues that are bombarding you at the same time … I love that laterality and having to see connections between seemingly unrelated events and actions'*

- **Relationships:** Building and maintaining relationships
  - o *'I gravitate towards certain sorts of people and with those other people I don't necessarily gel with, I make huge efforts to build and maintain those relationships, whether inside or outside work'*
  - o *'Success in business is all about relationships, it's critical … it's also critical in sport … relationships with team-mates, your relationship with your coaches'*
  - o *'The unique dynamic with others and the interactions … they need to be effective, the communication, the whole dynamic, I think, is really important to success'*

- **Humility:** Staying humble
  - o *'You're not the only one that matters … "we" is the key word'*
  - o *'Everybody's perspective is important'*
  - o *'It's really important, it gives people space to propose ideas and be excellent'*
  - o *'Humility is so important … you have to create the situation where people can feel comfortable telling you what they think or giving you their ideas … a lot of this comes from acknowledging that you might be the boss but that doesn't make you any better than them'*

Staying in tune with the environment requires agility in leaders so that they can react quickly to changing circumstances that often characterise top performance environments. Also important is the effort required in the building and maintenance of supportive relationships with people with whom they may not hit it off personally. Demonstrating humility is a key part of sustainable leadership in this respect because it enables leaders to have conversations with people who they recognise may have the answers they do not have themselves. It also creates an environment where people will 'tell it like it is' so that they are able to stay in tune with what is *really* happening around them.

Knowing how to deliver top performance

This final sustainable leadership know-how involves knowing how to deliver top performance which is sustainable and comprises three dimensions: 'preparation', 'delivery' and 'evaluation'. The specific areas of know-how underpinning these dimensions are shown in Figure 4.4.4.

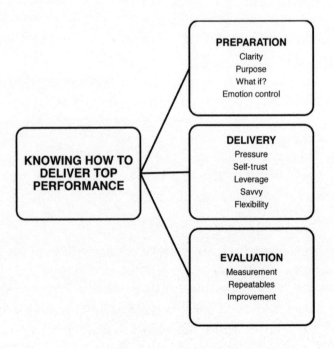

Figure 4.4.4 Knowing how to deliver top performance.

Preparation. Not surprisingly, preparing meticulously is a key aspect of sustained success and comprises:

- **Clarity:** Defining success
  - *'I prioritise the winning and the performance bits ... sometimes it's about winning and nothing else ... other times, it's about getting the performance right ... practising the bits that need to be right when it really matters and I need to raise my game ... and if I win, it's a bonus'*
  - *'You've always got to think about the bigger picture, the end goal, and the milestones along the way ... winning isn't always the most important thing'*
  - *'You know your game plan is better than the competition's and if you execute it, you know we'll win'*
  - *'Where was the competition this year and where will they be this time next year? ... that add-on factor as well'*
  - *'You may know what high performance is but you have to be sure your team knows as well'*

- **Purpose:** Making sure everything has a purpose
  - *'Everything you do should have a purpose ... if you have a vision and a plan then everything has a purpose, so what you do ends up being much more efficient'*
  - *'It's important not to get into the rut of going through the motions ... purposefulness is giving some thought to everything you do – what do I want to get out of it so that (a) I've achieved something and (b) it focuses me?'*

- **What if?:** Planning for every scenario
  - *'In my day we rehearsed game plans for different weather conditions until we knew them inside out'*
  - *'Before any big meeting I will always have a pre-brief or a run-through because it gives you and the team the opportunity to test*

> things … it's about second-guessing … one of the things we did at Company X was a "failure points analysis" … you always worked out what could go wrong and then you'd put it right before you did it so it didn't happen … it's about planning and preparing and is one of the most critical points of any success that I've had, trying to second-guess all the stuff that could go wrong and getting it right before you do it'

- **Emotion:** Optimising one's emotional state
  - 'I want to be totally present in the moment so I can respond to any challenge coming my way … there are rituals I'd go through to get myself into the right emotional state before a performance … if I missed some of those stages, I'm playing catch-up a little bit – I'm not saying I couldn't turn it on but it would be far more challenging'
  - 'When I've got that big presentation and a lot rests on it … I've got to wow them … I disappear during those final few minutes before and try to get into what I call my "control room" … I know what works for me, I want to be nervous but I want to be in control'
  - 'I know others who want to be as cool as ice but I'm at my best when I'm emotionally on fire'

Preparation begins with being clear about what success looks like. It is not always about winning and sustainable leadership know-how involves a deep understanding of the principles of outcome, output and input goals, described in Part 2.3, and how and when to set and implement them. Having people around who have a common perception and understanding of what top performance constitutes and what is required to deliver it is key to the sustainability of its achievement. Being clear about what success looks like means that leaders can be confident all activities have a common purpose and focus and time is not being wasted. And building in the 'what ifs' means overpreparing on the critical detail to help minimise surprises, panic and distraction when things do not go to plan. Finally, how leaders control and use their emotions is critical to getting the best out of themselves on a sustainable basis.

Delivery. This dimension comprises a number of aspects of delivering high performance on a sustainable basis:

- **Pressure:** Performing when it really matters
  - *'I'm at my best when it really matters'*
  - *'I have a mindset which is getting "nervous and excited" and not "nervous and scared"'*
  - *'Part of me says I cope but part of me says I get a big buzz out of pressure ... I get a buzz out of a million things coming at me that I've just got to deliver on ... I'm a pretty fast and lateral thinker and I get a huge adrenalin rush out of that'*
  - *'There's times when the intensity level is extremely high, when you're involved in important decisions, a key meeting, negotiating an acquisition ... you're at the height of emotions but at the same time have to maintain control, stay cool under pressure'*
  - *'Controlling what you're feeling, not letting that distract away from the job in hand, your focus, your preparation'*
  - *'Keeping calm, composed, and focused during critical high-pressure moments'*
  - *'It's about being able to maintain equilibrium and equanimity in the face of trials, challenge, distress and a whole raft of other things'*

- **Self-trust:** Letting it happen
  - *'Sometimes people get inhibited by fear ... no, not fear, they don't trust themselves in the moment ... I have a great trust of myself, I back myself in the moment'*
  - *'One of the fundamental ingredients of success is that you have faith in yourself and trust you can do this and just let it happen'*

- o *'It was intuitive when I was at my best on stage … it was amazing, I just let go and it just seemed to happen'*
- o *'Having the confidence to apply your intuition as a leader'*

- **Leverage:** Controlling the crucial controllables
  - o *'There's so much to do and so many initiatives I want to move forward … moving big organisations forward there's a couple of things you have to do really, really well rather than a lot of things halfway and have them take eighteen rather than nine months'*
  - o *'In cardiology you're focusing on the very specific problems of one particular patient and one particular disease that patient has and one specific procedure … nothing else matters'*

- **Savvy:** Seizing opportunities
  - o *'Making things happen to stay one step ahead of the competition'*
  - o *'Crystal-clear decision-making which enables you to increase performance … seize opportunities … that one critical crunch moment where the psychological momentum is either lost or gained, holding your nerve to seize that moment, and with consistency'*
  - o *'Having a savvy which involves a cleverness, knowing where the boundaries are and in-the-moment thinking that enables you to use them to your advantage'*
  - o *'The ability to deliver at a crunch time … being able to bring it all together in what might be a millisecond'*

- **Flexibility:** Knowing when to alter course
  - o *'Knowing when to stop persisting with Plan A because it isn't working or the conditions have changed, and knowing whether to implement Plan B or Plan C'*
  - o *'Knowing when to push and when to back off … there are times when you just have to accept it's not happening and come back and fight another day … and not pushing yourself so that you risk not being able to come back and fight another day'*

Not surprisingly, the ability to perform under pressure is critical to top performance leadership that is sustainable. Pressure is unavoidable and getting a buzz from it is a fundamental prerequisite for longevity in the role. This is facilitated by a robust trust in oneself and backing one's instinct and intuition. The ability to compartmentalise and focus on leveraging the crucial controllables was highlighted in Part 2.4 as important in regulating organisational performance, but it is clearly also a core aspect of Sustainable Leadership. It features prominently in the 'knowing how to work *with* the environment' aspect of Sustainable Leadership, but in that context is more about 'awareness' of the controllables as opposed to the 'leverage' of them to enable the delivery of top performance. Specific focus on leveraging the crucial controllables accompanied by the ability to remain calm, think clearly, make decisions and make things happen under pressure ensures that opportunities are seized rather than missed. It also means leaders have a flexibility which enables them to quickly recognise when executing the agreed plan is not the best course of action and to change things accordingly.

Evaluation. For top performance leadership to be sustainable, a process of evaluation is required, which forms the basis of continued growth and improvement. This final dimension comprises:

- **Measurement:** Comparing against measurement criteria
  - *'It's a very obvious thing to say but it keeps you on the straight and narrow … you need a good balance scorecard in place'*
  - *'I call it "watching the game film" … you have to know where you are and that means constant evaluation and stepping back to look at what's going on'*
  - *'Always go back to the detailed goals you set in the planning stage … which goals did you hit, which didn't you hit?'*

- ○ *'I believe that we shouldn't just be looking at processes or outputs but outcomes … outcomes being lives saved or unwanted births prevented and things like that. If you push through the boundaries of what you evaluate … so you're not just evaluating efficiency or processes … too many people evaluate a snapshot of today instead of benchmarking that against what could or should be and what it's going to lead to tomorrow'*

- **Repeatables:** Picking out the good bits
  - ○ *'People too often forget to celebrate the bits that went well and to learn from them'*
  - ○ *'You need to notice the good stuff every day'*
  - ○ *'It's too easy to focus only on what you can't do or what isn't going well and forget that there is a lot going well too … it's not about "today was a great day" … it should be "what was great about it?" … really getting into the detail so that you repeat the good stuff again and again'*

- **Improvement:** Identifying what needs work
  - ○ *'How would we do it better next time? … it stops you getting complacent'*
  - ○ *'This isn't about beating yourself up … that serves no useful purpose … it's about that constant urge to do things even better next time … to keep moving forward so that you stay ahead of the competition'*
  - ○ *'Gives me that short-term focus and motivation that keeps me going, day after day'*

Performance is not the end point for leaders with sustainable leadership know-how. Sustained success equals continually seeking and forensically evaluating ways to move to the next level. Comparing against measurement criteria emphasises the importance of a detailed assessment of performance based on goals and benchmarks, which enable progress to be monitored in the longer-term. There always seem to be aspects of performance that 'need work' and improvement, even if it is just to prevent complacency creeping in, but this know-how also involves 'picking out the good bits' so that they are reinforced and replicable.

Conclusion

Sustainable Leadership is the key to enabling leaders to integrate their inner motive to be *real* with the demands of the broader external environment. Top performance leaders' strength and depth in all three know-hows underpins their sustainability and longevity. 'Knowing how to self-actualise' equips them with a self-knowledge and ability to self-regulate which drives both resilience and personal growth. 'Knowing how to work *with* the environment' helps them to lead their people more effectively, as well as enabling them to shape the environment to their advantage so that their path to self-actualisation is as smooth as possible. Finally, 'knowing how to deliver top performance' provides them with the ability to deliver the goods on a sustainable basis.

4.5 Summary

I emphasised early on in this book that top performance leadership is not about skills so this is not a text on *how* to lead. Instead, top performance leadership is about the motives, support and know-how, and how they are directed, used and adapted to create, maintain and continually enhance the environment that will deliver top performance.

Real Leadership is not really about what leaders do but much more about the mindset and behaviours that form the foundation of having the confidence to let go, being willing to make mistakes, having the courage to make and own tough decisions, having the conviction to do the right thing and accepting accountability when things go wrong.

Team Leadership involves creating a top performance team and requires understanding, patience and skill on the part of the leader but the rewards of getting it right are considerable. Top performance leaders have a team around them who are good and passionate about what they do, accountable and reliable and, above all, loyal. This is the very support required by top performance leaders.

Sustainable Leadership brings with it a requirement for powerful personal resources in the form of resilience, strength of character, optimism balanced with realism and self-belief. These will aid Sustainable Leadership and continued growth, but knowing how to turn the environment to the leader's advantage and, crucially, how to deliver the performance expected and demanded are also necessary.

Part 5

Top Performance Leadership in Action

5.1 Looking to others' experiences

I described in the Introduction how I have been keen to subject the PEL Model at the core of this book to validation by people who collectively represent a broad range of experience and expertise across a variety of performance settings. The five people comprising the Advisory Board have already shaped the content of this book by providing feedback on the working manuscript as it evolved. These people were also asked to provide an independent written commentary on the PEL Model and its applicability to the organisations and sectors they have worked in. Their commentaries appear in the section that follows. Figure 5.1.1 provides an overview of the core components of the model, together with the various aspects and elements underpinning each, which have formed the detailed content of this book.

Top performance leaders start by defining the performance to be delivered: the what?, why?, who?, when? and how? They then oversee the creation of the environment and conditions in which their people can thrive and deliver top performance. Following this, they then focus on applying their *real*, team and sustainable leadership skills and know-how to ensure the delivery of top performance.

The Advisory Board's commentaries feature below, in which they share examples and insights that reinforce and bring the model to life, as well as highlighting other aspects of the book's content that have particularly resonated with them.

PERFORMANCE

Define the What? Why?
Who? When? How?

Define:
Create visions that work
Define outputs, outcomes and impact
Identify CPIs
Design:
Set outcome, output and input goals
Manage performance tensions
Deliver:
Regulate performance
Balance effectiveness and efficiency

ENVIRONMENT

Create the conditions in
which people can thrive

Focus:
Get the achievement, processes,
innovation and well-being focus 'just
right'
Vision, challenge *and* support:
Ensure all are present
Enablers:
Ensure incentives, information and
instruments are in place
People:
Be clear about the capacity, mindset and
behaviours required

LEADERSHIP

Ensure the delivery of
sustainable top performance

Real:
Make things happen for the right reasons
Team:
Inspire, unite and align people to become
a top performance team
Sustainable:
Know how to self-actualise
Know how to work *with* the environment
Know how to deliver top performance

Figure 5.1.1 Top performance leadership: An overview.

5.2 Advisory Board's commentaries

Dr Jonathan Goldman MD (JG)

Jonathan is executive VP of Business Development at ICON Clinical Research in San Francisco. A fellow of the American College of Cardiology and the Royal College of Physicians, he also maintains a Faculty appointment as an associate clinical professor of medicine at the University of California and serves as attending cardiologist at the San Francisco Veterans Administration Medical Center.

My experiences of leadership span the spectrum of the fields of clinical medicine as a consultant physician, in a biotechnology company as a C Level executive and in a pharmaceutical services public company as head of business development. Each of these professional spheres has different performance objectives and measures of success. The practice of medicine by the healthcare team, led by the physician, is directed towards the care of the individual patient in the environment of a hospital. Although the medical team will measure success in terms of mortality rates, alleviation of symptoms and reduced complication rates, the hospital will itself attempt to make a profit (or at least minimise financial losses). The physician leader of the team has to be part of both worlds and manage expectations of patients and staff where available resources are limited, resulting in waiting lists and sometimes sub-optimal care. This presents unique leadership challenges where the medical team is responsible for sicker patients. A biotechnology company and its employees must innovate and succeed in its research projects or it will not survive. For profit public companies empower senior executives to manage their teams to drive growth and profitability. The fundamental elements of the 'performance – environment – leadership' model that are core to this book correspond to issues that emerge in all of these sectors.

This book emphasises the importance of teambuilding, team working and impact in top performance leadership. I will never forget my first day working as an intern in a large hospital with many complex sick patients and how overwhelmed I felt with the demands and responsibilities of my new position. I could tell from the faces of my fellow interns how others felt the same. All of us were surprised to receive pager messages from the senior physician in charge of the department inviting us for tea and cakes with him and the senior nursing team in one of the offices. We all sat and talked about the history of the hospital (over 1,000 years old!) and the great physicians who had trained there over the years. We left the room and went back to our gruelling jobs hugely uplifted by the sense of being part of the history of an institution.

When reading the manuscript, I was drawn to Graham's distinction between 'real' and 'safe' leaders and as I look back twenty-five years later, I see the senior physician's efforts that day as a clear example of *real leadership*. He was prepared to take a risk and spend his own time during the most stressful period of a new career to focus us on what was important in the longer-term. A *safe* leader could have simply reviewed the list of tasks and activities to be performed, which although important, would have further increased stress for the team. His efforts were essentially intended to define expectations of performance, raise awareness about the environment we were responsible for creating and then build a team to lead and deliver it. He was unknowingly guiding us through the PEL Model on which this book is based, as well as instilling a sense of belonging with the message, 'You are part of the team that has done this important role in this institution for hundreds of years, and all of them have gone through what you are currently experiencing.'

I tried to adopt similar techniques when building my Research and Development team as a chief medical officer in an early stage biotechnology company. This was my first experience of leading a team that was based remotely, which was tasked with supervising the conduct of a large and challenging multi-centre clinical trial of a highly innovative product. The team was required to travel long hours and supervise some very technical aspects. I was able to unite the team around the importance of their individual contributions, such that if the programme were successful the drug would be available for the benefit of millions of patients with heart disease. In the book, Graham emphasises the importance of viewing performance not just as an 'output' or 'outcome' but rather what he describes as its 'impact'. Getting my team to focus on the impact rather than just the output of their hard work had a positive effect on the performance environment in terms of their mindsets and behaviours.

Most recently, I have experienced the challenges of leading a global sales function for a large public company. Everyone in the sales organisation, including myself, has numerical goals that define success and which obviously need to be achieved to ensure the successful growth of the firm. I organised the group into teams with goals that aligned each individual with team and corporate goals, such that the success of other team members, under certain circumstances, lead to rewards for team-mates. This has resulted in a change in culture from 'me' to 'us' that has improved morale and performance and reinforces Graham's assertions in the book that leaders should focus on and devote quality time to identifying goals that are totally aligned. It is so important to get this right because it impacts greatly on the environment.

Leadership is about continuing to perform at the top after one has got there. Graham associates 'sustainable leadership' with the ability of a leader to 'self-actualise' and to 'work *with* rather than *against* the environment', as well as 'knowing how to deliver top performance'. My personal experience in clinical medicine included constant external testing of knowledge in daily life/death decision-making, coupled with similarly constant feedback from patients, peers, support staff and superiors on performance. I concur with the premise that emotional and intellectual resilience is necessary for growth, since mistakes are inevitable and with feedback you can grow. The book further emphasises the need to be aware of your environment (both internal to your company and among your marketplace); I have found that this sensitivity allows better analysis of leading indicators of change in sentiment among employees and customers alike. The sustainable leader can therefore always look forward, rather than backwards.

Finally, perhaps most important in delivering top performance is to be aware that details really do matter. Graham encourages leaders to leave nothing to chance and he is absolutely correct. I have found that the leadership role in industry is not that different from directing the care of patients in an intensive care unit; time spent on critically reviewing data in real time, deciding what is important and what is not, what advice is useful and what is not, helps decide the optimal course of action. These are the characteristics of a top performance leader.

Graham Hodgkin (GH)

Graham is CEO of London's Air Ambulance and was formerly a managing director at Deutsche Bank in London, with responsibility for the Corporate Banking Coverage function, in addition to his role as UK & Ireland country head for the Global Transaction Bank.

Perhaps my individual journey is somewhat atypical and gives me a different lens on leadership in a number of sectors and roles. Having spent twenty-five years in financial services, starting pretty much at the bottom in a clerical role within operations and ending up as a country head and managing director for one of the world's most successful and recognisable investment banking brands, I have both witnessed and been subjected to myriad leadership styles and traits, all of which have informed my own thoughts and behaviours as I have grown in influence and impact. Within that, I have built successful businesses in the boom times and tried to sustain them in the midst of the greatest global financial crisis in living memory.

That latter experience alone highlighted some of the critical components within Graham's book, notably: the importance of 'real' leadership (versus the perceived acceptability of 'safe' leadership when economies are growing, confidence is high and shareholders are satisfied); the need to focus on selected and targeted Critical Performance Indicators; and the necessity of paying close attention to the process of performance itself.

I witnessed first-hand 'safe' leaders completely lose their way, themselves and ultimately their status whilst seeing some 'real' leaders emerge, who were in tune with their environment (to the extent that anybody could be at that time), who were capable of self-actualisation and who understood the importance of internal communications, both structured and in the corridors.

Three years on, and having transitioned through establishing and running my own consultancy practice, I am well into my latest career phase as a CEO for a small but high-profile London-based charity that is in the business of providing life-saving care to critically injured people, quite literally on the streets of England's capital city. I have endeavoured to overlay Graham's thoughts and observations around the topics of leadership and indeed top performance as I have taken on this role.

I have no medical, aviation or direct social-sector experience and yet I have been amazed by the degree of transformation that we have achieved during my tenure, which has reaffirmed my passion and belief in the topics that Graham discusses in this book. We have reignited the vision for the organisation, agreed new overarching values that will inform our behaviours and created top-performance frameworks to nurture, measure and sustain those behaviours. We have spent significant time on resourcing the charity with the right people, doing the right things and with an appropriate balance between structure and process, innovation and autonomy. Ours is an organisation that genuinely saves lives, whilst incurring significant risk, underpinned by a relentless focus on governance, quality and the performance of the team, all of which is conducted in extreme and often harrowing circumstances. Poor resource allocation, a high degree of short-termism, and people or teams that do not have resilience and/or a strong sense of belonging are just some of the dangers that Graham highlights which could have terrible consequences for our future patients.

Whilst Graham's writing is predominantly research-based, he has an incredible ability to effectively unpick the demanding world of leadership and to articulate his key messages in a clear way that encourages us as the reader to both understand and relate to the issues and pitfalls, whilst offering solutions and tools that enable us to keep moving forward with a renewed sense of purpose. Such tools are complemented by supporting prompts for us to stay focused on the future and the external factors that Graham identifies as potentially so impactful. His ability to both integrate and articulate his performance models, and to effectively aggregate internal and external factors with short- and long-term horizons, whilst demanding that appropriate time and energy is expended on creating the right environment within which our people can rightly flourish, is very compelling and powerful.

Of course, the ultimate goal is sustainable top performance and I genuinely believe Graham's book helps us to be aware of the barriers and to provide means to mitigate the challenges whilst providing invaluable support, guidance and direction to enable us to face them all with a heightened degree of perception, motivation and confidence.

Ultimately, I remain passionate about the role of leadership and its correlation to top performance. I am now further convinced that as leaders, we have an absolute responsibility to at least endeavour to do the right thing and to constantly and consistently role-model the behaviours and values that we determine are the 'non-negotiables' for ourselves and the organisations that we have the privilege to lead. The transition that Graham describes from solely outputs and outcomes to impact deeply resonates with. Having now reflected on his book, that is where I intend to focus more of my energies as I try to take my organisation to the next level, and as I embrace sustainable and real leadership to the extent that I can.

John Peters (JP)

John started his career as an RAF fast jet pilot and was shot down, held as a prisoner of war and paraded on TV during the first Gulf War in 1991. During the remainder of his RAF career, he continued to fly and finished his service in the MOD, responsible for programmes on leadership, performance and safety culture in aviation. In 2000, he retired from the RAF and has since consulted on leadership, strategy and change in a broad range of organisations as managing director of his own company, Monkey Business.

Let me start with a question. Are you a good driver? On a scale of performance from 1 to 10, how would you rate your driving abilities compared to other drivers on the road? Simple question, but over the years when asking groups of senior managers, MBA students and talent groups in many businesses, it is quite amazing – usually I get scores between 6 and 10; rarely a 5, mostly 7 or 8, and I fall off my perch if I get a 4 or less. So I stand before you lucky enough to work with the top-end performers of driving ability in the population. Or do I?

We all may *believe* that we are high performers, but the reality is probably very different. It demonstrates our bias towards a *sense* of our own ability rather than the brutal truth of our *real* ability. The probability is that given all the managers with whom I have worked over the years, they probably reflect the population and vary between 1 and 10, whether they believe it or not! This same reflection applies to performance in all organisations and, in particular, to leaders. Please do not take offence. I get it – we all like to believe we work with 'the best'; that there is something truly unique about our organisation that separates us from the norm;

that we 'must be good' because we are in the talent group or work in a 'world-class' organisation, but all these judgements are relative.

This judgement of performance is also comparative, because do you know how you lead compared to contemporaries in similar roles with similar experience, both within and outside your business or sector? Many may believe that they are leaders and instinctively feel they perform their role well, but often the reality is very different. They may believe it to be so and that their challenges are unique, but this may not be the case. And thank goodness for that, or else I would not have a business! Corporate leaders talk about it, talk leadership up, talk of its importance and initiate leadership workshops, but a sustained performance-improving *practice* is rare – they are just too busy! But, if we are to believe all the research, such as the 2009 Gallup poll, which suggested that leadership makes a 30 per cent difference to the discretionary effort that people give the business, surely our high performers should be putting sustained practice into improving their leadership skills. Note the key words in the Gallup poll: 'discretionary' and 'give'. Most businesses could not operate without the extra effort that we all provide – hence why 'work-to-rule' brings businesses to a resounding halt. By corollary, this is why top performance leaders are so valued – they make a difference to the sustained performance of the organisation.

So what can we do about it? Well, Graham hits the nail on the head – he fuses performance with leadership and he knows what he is talking about. He provides tools for enabling leaders to actually transform their performance through a series of simple, though not simplistic, concepts and models that will enhance their leadership ability. Of course, these are not quick fixes. Coming from a high-performance sport psychology background, he knows only too well that even Olympians cannot just go from national to world-class without practice. Of course, they are blessed with natural talent, but if they want a gold medal they have to train relentlessly for four years just to increase their performance by the slightest of margins to attain world-class. And it is not just about improving upon their technique, physicality and nutritional needs – it includes training mindset and attitude to overcome their habitual approach in order to set up new rituals of excellence to attain that required performance. So, if you truly believe you are a top performance leader, you will not be assuming that through the nature of your high-powered position with its demanding responsibilities, impressive title and your strength of character that you will naturally acquire these skills *just* by doing your job. With an authentic performance approach, you will be fusing this experience with Graham's advice to break through unconscious biases, setting up new rituals and evolving your abilities so that you truly realise new levels of performance as a leader.

This approach is reflected in flying high-performance combat fighter aircraft, where Graham's simple model works very well. The performance defines the environment which, in turn, defines the leadership; it is a balance between practising and optimising combat abilities within the boundaries of safety, risk and return, but close enough to combat realities so that, come mobilisation for such a scenario, aircrew can push their limits of performance to that ultimate level. The resulting leadership involves balancing the need for combat effectiveness within peacetime constraints (environmental, safety, cost, risk and political) to the requirements of wartime performance. Performance defines everything, especially when one is operating at the edges of performance. Air combat involves pilots flying right on the edge of failure. In terms of the physics of the aircraft, the maximum performance (the maximum rate of turn, the critical element in air combat) is a whisper away from the edge of failure – pull only to 98 per cent of maximum performance and the other aircraft will out-turn you, shoot you down and you are dead; pull a whisper past the maximum rate of turn and the airflow washes off your wings, the aircraft drops from the sky and the other aircraft will shoot you down or you crash. Concurrently, the pilot is operating at the limits of human physiology – high G literally sucks the blood from one's head. At high G, pilots are playing with their consciousness, fighting to keep the blood in their heads whilst completing complex manoeuvres, engaging in intricate systems management through HOTAS (hands on throttle and stick) whilst under the intense workload of managing fuel consumption (in afterburner – tanks dry is less than five minutes!), navigation, ground threats and maintaining situational awareness.

To maintain the raft of necessary skills requires constructing an authentic performance environment that Graham advocates. The environment and, subsequently, the leadership are set up to maximise learning. Every sortie is about maximising the learning to expose and improve upon each other's weaknesses. It is planning to learn; briefing to learn and de-briefing what we have learned – relentlessly – *every* trip. Debriefing even the slightest deviation away from perfection, even despite the fact that nowadays the computer will correct the error! But that is not the point. It is an environment of performance; it is an attitude of mind.

Fighter pilots are not confident because they tell each other how good they are; they are confident because they expose themselves to critical peer review every day of their careers. No matter what rank is in the debriefing room. Outside the debriefing, rank is respected;

inside each pilot is just another professional trying to be the best s/he can be. Of interest, most squadron commanders by that stage of their careers will not be the best pilot in the room, nor do they need to be. Their job is to set the environment. Everyone leading by example; the best example their experience can provide and sharing their knowledge to improve one another within a competitive but collaborative process. It is the realisation that the potential enemy, ultimately, is working to expose these very same weaknesses! Hence, there is no room for sensitivities – it is the performance that matters; learning is everything.

And the brutal reality is that the results and figures do not lie. No offence is taken: the leadership required is to maintain a competitive, challenging atmosphere within a vigorous shared learning environment; all whilst creating the human connection, esprit de corps and morale that is *the* essential competitive advantage in any military unit. Of course, I understand that a fighter squadron is a very specific role, requiring very specific skills to attain specific results. I am not advocating the direct style or approach, but the environment of leading by example and the principles of a performance-led learning culture are reflected throughout Graham's advocacy for top performance leadership. The performance defines the environment, which defines the leadership: top down, bottom up. It is a culture that I have rarely come across in business.

So I could close by asking, are you evolving as a leader? Do you have a strategy for improving your leadership? To conclude, however, that really is not the answer to the question! As Graham establishes early on, the answer is – it is not about you! It is about your ability to enable *others* to be top performers. Now that is a top performance leader. So what are you going to do about it?

Dominic Sheldrick (DS)

Dom is the MD of Picline Performance Consultants based in Perth, Australia, and has worked closely with leaders in organisations, which include Deutsche Bank, BP, Roche Pharmaceuticals, J.P. Morgan, Coca-Cola and Minter Ellison. He swam for Australia during the 1980s.

As a retired elite athlete and now performance development consultant over the past twenty years in Australia, the UK and Asia, I have spent a lot of time conversing with business leaders and sports people about the key challenges associated with performing at higher and higher levels as a leader to satisfy themselves and the various stakeholders they impact. If my career were to end today, I would be left with a consistent picture in my mind of leaders in varying states of (mostly hidden) anxiety about what they are doing, how they are doing it and why they are doing what they do, because their leadership impact seems so subjective and open to interpretation. Having reflected on those many conversations recently, I would contend that many leaders have been in some way convinced it is their tireless efforts that can alone make the difference between 'good' and 'great' performance. This belief has resulted in many of the leaders I interact with being on a never-ending treadmill of effort to get their business to perform.

A key realisation for me is that just focusing on improved leadership is not the panacea for the never-ending challenges faced by leaders today. The challenge is to take a closer look at the current orthodoxy where most of us view the following continuum to be true: leadership impacts on the environment, which impacts on performance. At first glance, this seems reasonable and rational, but this book encourages us to turn it on its head and argues that leaders must look to inform their strategies by first asking what performance is required and then asking themselves (and others) what environment is required to deliver this performance. This argument that we must put leadership last and allow performance and the environment to inform The Why, The How and The What of leadership became increasingly compelling as I progressed through the book.

I now realise that this is actually what played out in the most powerful experience I had as an athlete pursuing my dream of swimming for my country as a nineteen-year-old national-level swimmer. Until this point I was ill-focused, ill-disciplined and wasting the talent that I had been blessed with. As much as a way to get out of going to university as it was to be the best swimmer I could be, I won a scholarship to attend the world-famous Australian Institute of Sport (AIS). Once 'on campus' I very quickly became aware that I was totally outside my comfort zone in coming from a club-based programme where I was the 'big fish' to a programme that boasted several Olympic and Commonwealth Games medallists and Australian Champions.

My overriding memory was the focus on performance whilst at the AIS, but not the usual general air of performance focus I often find in the corporate world; this was *my* performance and what *I* needed to achieve. My coach was both intense and curious in helping me to define why I was doing this and what I wanted to achieve. He would encourage me to dream a little and to write down what I *really* wanted, and then meet with me one-on-one to discuss what this meant for me. He was extremely thorough about helping me to define what needed to take place, and by when, to fulfil my ambition. He would 'investigate' this with me until I had a clear picture in my head of the conditions that would allow me to think purposefully about what I would focus on and how I would behave to give me the best chance to deliver on my ambitions. This detailed approach to what is described in this book as 'defining and designing performance' is exactly what my coach did with me. The impact was that every hour and every minute of my day had meaning. Put simply, I knew why I got out of bed in the morning, why I chose to eat what I did, why I chose to stay home instead of party, why I focused on the technique instead of accepting mediocrity; essentially, I saw the links between the outcomes I desired and the attitude, beliefs and the process-orientated behaviours which became the building blocks to my success.

In my experience in the corporate sector I have seen far too many leaders and team members negatively impacted by stress and anxiety because of their inability to create the required clarity about the performance that is desired. Rather, they exist in environments where leaders push teams hard in ways that may not necessarily be conducive to producing the performance that to many remains invisible.

With this focus during my time at the AIS, within twelve weeks a massive transformation had occurred. I had just swum at my second Open National Championships and had been selected to represent Australia for the first time when only six months prior (at my first Nationals) I had failed to make the final. In making this national team, it was apparent to me that I felt very different to any other time in my life. The usual 'high' levels of performance anxiety I felt during both training and racing were not present. The ability to think calmly about and alter the way in which I behaved was very palpable, and the attitudes I had towards competing and training were vastly (positively) altered. Reflecting on why and how this occurred leads me to contemplate the environment that had been carefully constructed at the AIS, including the physical infrastructure, the personnel, the programme, the support staff, the constant feedback and availability of performance-related information and testing, and the impact that this had on my ability to perform. It became apparent that the focus on performance in combination with the bespoke environment helped me to move from 'hoping and praying' to 'knowing and expecting' my performances would be what I had defined they should be. To be more explicit, as described in this book, the environment considered more than just achievements and outputs; it considered the well-being of the athlete and the innovative approaches to technique, diet, relaxation and conditioning, and it also acknowledged an individualised process orientation towards how things got done for each athlete.

My experience within organisations leads me to believe that (mostly unknowingly) the focus within the environment is mostly orientated towards profit, loss, earnings, budgets, targets, etc., and does not fully link the development and engagement of human capital, fostering an environment of innovation and development of processes which support the outcomes required.

As a natural developer of human potential, my coach was very much focused on how he could bring out the best in others; this is what gave him a huge sense of personal pride and achievement. He was focused on helping me to be aware and in control of the performance I needed/wanted from myself at any given point in my development as an athlete. The impact that he had on me was that he immediately and enduringly made me feel that I belonged to his team. He was unwaveringly positive and held each of his team members in the highest possible regard; he saw greatness in each of us to the point where I started to develop a more positive and healthy regard for my strengths and attributes. Most powerfully, he was able to tap into my intrinsic motivation by helping me to realise the impact of taking personal accountability and responsibility for my own actions as an athlete. I can remember him saying to me, 'Dom, I can't swim the race for you so it doesn't matter what I think, it matters what *you* think.'

The simple and uncluttered definition my coach held as to what his role should be was the most striking attribute about him, and his simple tenet of 'I can't swim the race for you' was the mindset that drove everything he did in preparing his athletes to be the best they could be. I realised as I read this book that he saw his role as the leader to be what Graham describes as 'create the conditions for people to thrive'. He was supremely comfortable in himself as a human being, evidenced by the joy that others got from their performance. Success was always measured in his athletes' results much more than it ever was about him. He was totally focused on us as human beings with our unique qualities and attributes. He focused appropriately on the future and on 'the now' in times of potential stress or performance anxiety. My memory is of an unrelenting positivity founded on a belief he 'chose' to have about the potential of every human being to be better today than they were yesterday. He had an ego which allowed us to explore different options, techniques and programmes, and encouraged us to speak with as many coaches, trainers, dietitians, doctors, biomechanists and the like to ensure we had the best possible environment to be the best we could be. As I read the section in the book emphasising the importance of humility in 'sustainable leadership', my mind immediately turned to my coach.

I have experienced this type of leader as a rare commodity in other performance settings. Too often, leaders are focused on being such great leaders and showing the world what great leaders they can be that they miss the simple things that can make their working lives so much more fulfilling, which can also impact upon their organisations in ways that produce engaged people in environments where these people are focused on delivering what the organisation says it will.

Sue White (SW)

Sue is a group HR director and global HR business leader who has spent twenty-five years leading HR teams and business partnering with leaders at the highest level in United Technology Corporation, Alstom SA, Peugeot SA, Johnson Controls Automotive and Jaguar Cars Ltd.

Being a life-long learner, HR leader and in industry for over twenty-five years, I have an office full of books on business, strategy, HR management practice, leadership and organisational development. So it was with very little hesitation that I accepted Graham's invitation to read and comment on the manuscript of this, his latest book. What I did not bargain on when I asked what the book was about was for him to say modestly, 'Performance and leadership'. I have to admit my next thought was, 'Why does business need any more books on performance and leadership?'

Well, I could not have been more wrong. Put simply, Graham has managed to nail the profile and development of the outstanding leader as 'real' versus 'safe', as well as turn leadership on its head to enable leaders to create the best environment necessary to achieve outstanding and sustainable top performance. At the same time, he has also answered the question of why, in my role of HR director, I have found myself having to re-engineer, refresh and relaunch the annual performance review process in the first twelve to twenty-four months in nearly every business I have joined. Let me illustrate what I mean with a few examples.

Firstly, I believe one of the most challenging stages in any senior leader's career path to the boardroom is when one shifts from leading a team in close proximity in a single location to leading team members and multiple teams across several geographical locations, often in different countries and across continents. The criteria for success in this scenario, in my opinion, is what Graham would describe as 'real'. When reading the section on 'safe' versus 'real' leadership I found myself reflecting fondly on the years in which I business partnered with one of the most visionary, inspiring and compelling leaders I have ever worked with. At great personal risk, this leader had taken on a very high-profile global opportunity, mid-career and in an unproven market, to build a new service division for a global transport and energy Original Equipment Manufacturer and market leader. In addition, he was succeeding a previous leader who had moved on after only six months in the role. By believing in the impossible, hiring the right talent, inspiring and believing in global and local visions, this CEO worked tirelessly with his team and in forensic detail to bring the vision to reality.

Having reflected on Graham's work, I am reminded of the benefit of spending days in strategy and planning workshops in countries all over the world, poring over layers of detail to define performance outcomes and outputs with our regional business teams. I learned to 'trust the process' and understood that 'the devil is in the detail'. The most thrilling moment in my career was when we launched and co-facilitated our first 'leading and managing in times of change' communications workshop, engaging first the top 100 and ultimately the top 300 leaders to become part of a new global organisation and transport service culture, all versed in leading change and delivering the vision.

This leader, whom I now recognise as 'real', has since moved on to the world of non-executive directorships to spread the word. He was recognised in 2012 by *The Times* for a Private Equity Award for Non-Executive Directors and named as 'The Chief Psychology Officer'. His legacy as a 'real' leader is a source of inspiration and will remain with those with whom we worked for many years to come.

The second example emanates from my business-partner role with leaders, normally in one of two scenarios. Either the brief is to deliver a major change programme or we are new in position, inheriting an executive team and transitioning businesses to re-define performance in terms of profitability and top-line growth. What has always intrigued, and if I am honest, frustrated me, is why in the second scenario I have arrived in position to find the company's prevailing performance management process to be completely ineffective in terms of alignment, relevance, delivery of results and sustainability. More often than not, there is nothing wrong with the tool itself; however, I can now conclude that in most cases these issues could all have been avoided had sufficient attention been paid to detail at the outset by way of 'definition, design and delivery' of what *it* is that was to be achieved in terms of performance. This is my own impactful learning, which is so well captured in this book in Graham's 3D Model of Top Performance.

I believe this argument is strengthened even further when someone with my experience of large change programmes looks to how well we do define *it* in terms of vision or desired future state, outcomes, outputs and impact for a change programme. As well as paying close attention to how the project will be managed in terms of the criteria for success in the environment, we re-engineer processes and select the right talent to deliver against clearly defined goals. For me, Graham has hit the nail on the head here by suggesting to leaders that they 'put performance first'.

My final example relates to my personal experience as a HR leader when, with hindsight, I had the opportunity and realised the creation of a top performance environment. Five years ago, in the context of a major (£1.2bn) business acquisition and integration in the fire and security service sector, I was asked to create a new 'best-in-class' HR organisation and team to be founded on the principles of field-based HR business partners, transactional shared services and specialist in-house recruitment, learning and development resources. My modest personal recollection of this organisational achievement has always been to recognise the talented people with whom I had the pleasure to work, who in turn have praised our collective vision of what 'great' would look like and complimented me as a leader on my enthusiasm, energy and support. However, our collective success was far more than that.

Looking back on it, all four elements identified in this book necessary to create a top performance environment – focus, the balance across vision/challenge/support, enablers and people – came together to facilitate a great outcome, which was recognised globally:

- *Focus.* HR partnered with business operations at the organisation, team and individual level to generate alignment of what 'great' would look like in support of the business achieving its goals. Focus was on quality in the form of a detailed quality policy and processes, cost in terms of a detailed set of metrics and KPIs, and delivery through a detailed internal service level agreement.
- *Vision, challenge and support.* A clearly articulated and detailed *vision* was developed by all stakeholders to define the desired

future state. The team deployed gated project management criteria to test the robustness of delivery at every stage and *challenged* themselves by external benchmarking to continuously improve the process. *Support* took the form of personal development plans, programmes and role opportunities to facilitate retention and progression. By acquiring new skills and completing HR qualifications, people could grow as the organisation matured and grew in scope.

- *Enablers.* Whilst the initial start-up to go-live was only three months, three work streams ran in parallel over three years to design, develop, implement, refine and scale: process, technology and people-related requirements. Investment in new technology in the form of an integrated system with state-of-the-art call-centre telephony benefited not only automation for greater efficiency, it also engaged the line managers in transacting the process and contributed to retention and hiring of HR talent to support growth as the team expanded their scope across all business units in the UK.

- *People.* An extremely talented team was formed from the Legacy Company, as well as new hires with a strong track record of experience in what we wanted to achieve. It was vital that everyone shared the same values to create and agree a vision and extremely detailed definition of what 'great' would look like in terms of operational plans to deliver outstanding future performance. The team defined and was committed to a set of customer 'service-excellence' organisation design principles, which underlined robust decision-making along the way.

Outstanding and sustained levels of performance can still be observed five years later as this team continues to deliver and outperform expectation and targets in terms of quality, cost and delivery. They have achieved 'silver status' as assessed by the corporate program of Achieving Competitive Excellence and are well on the journey to gold, being recognised globally as an in-house reference for HR shared services and regularly benchmarked by other country HR teams. It is hard to imagine life in this business before 'HRFirst' became a reality. Here is a great example of putting everything that Graham advocates in place to create a top performance environment: we got the focus right; we got the correct balance across providing vision, challenge and support; we put the appropriate enablers in place; and we ensured we had people in place with the necessary ability and mindsets.

These are only three examples of the many I could have shared which validate the relevance and added value of the PEL Model. It goes to show that there is definitely room on the shelf for another book on performance and leadership and I wish I had had access to this invaluable resource much earlier in my leadership career.

5.3 Summary

These commentaries testify to the wide applicability of the PEL Model across the broad-ranging performance settings represented by the Advisory Board. Despite different objectives and measures of success across large business organisations, the Third Sector, military, sport and medicine, as JP emphatically states, 'performance defines everything'. Indeed, it is interesting that DS now realises that it was the PEL approach adopted by his coach that underpinned his success as an international swimmer. And JG tells the story of how he was part of the clinical team in a major hospital where, in hindsight, the leader took great care in ensuring the team was clear about what it was tasked with achieving, the environment required to achieve it and how this drove the leadership and teamwork required. This was the PEL Model in action.

Emerging from the commentaries are potential detrimental consequences for leaders who continue to put their leadership ahead of performance and the environment. DS talks about the vulnerability of leaders and the anxiety caused by uncertainty about what their role actually is. This is exacerbated in leaders who are also convinced that it is their 'tireless efforts' alone that can make the key difference to performance; these leaders carry a heavy burden indeed. Even worse is when they impose what DS refers to as a 'treadmill of effort' on their teams and push them too hard to deliver something that is unclear because they have never achieved sufficient clarity on what it is they are trying to deliver. JP alerts us to leaders who may wrongly believe they are doing all of the things covered in this book, whilst DS has seen leaders who are so focused on showing what great leaders they are that they miss the simple things; it is these simple things that can make the difference! Complacency in some leaders and ignorance in others stems from putting their leadership first and results in an environment in which key enablers are either absent, inappropriate or poorly implemented.

The importance of putting performance first comes through loud and clear in the commentaries. GH emphasises the importance of paying attention to the process of performance, highlighting the identification of the vision, performance impact and CPIs as being core to taking his organisation to the next level. JG reinforces the importance of identifying performance 'impact' in addition to 'output' and 'outcome' and how this had a positive effect on the mindsets and behaviours in a team he led. He also highlights the efficacy of aligning individual, team and organisational goals. SW talks about how devoting attention to the necessary 'forensic' detail in defining, designing and delivering performance (the 3D Model of Top Performance), and identifying a clear vision in particular, means that potential issues in performance management are prevented later on. JG raises the leadership challenge of accommodating and managing performance tensions, describing what are effectively conflicting KPIs in hospitals, where physician leaders are faced with saving lives and helping the hospital hit budget at the same time. GH similarly highlights the need to manage performance tensions effectively, warning of the dangers of short-termism and the need to focus on future sustainability by balancing internal and external factors with short- and long-term horizons.

An important learning point for leaders in all performance settings emerges from DS's commentary in which he describes how being clear about what he was trying to achieve transformed his mindset, behaviours and his whole approach to his swimming. Importantly, the clarity which his coach helped him achieve actually reduced his performance anxiety. This is powerful testimony indeed for the need to put performance first.

With performance clearly defined, the Advisory Board, without exception, are in agreement that the leader's role is, as GH describes it, to 'create the environment where people can flourish'. DS tells how his coach went to great lengths to create the environment where the potential he looked for and saw in his swimmers could be realised. JP refers to the leader's role as balancing a challenging competitive atmosphere with a supportive learning one, emphasising the importance of providing both challenge *and* support.

Fundamental to achieving the top performance environment is attention to detail. I alerted you at the beginning of Part 4 to the numerous layers of detail that leaders need to consider and that you, as a reader, would be asked to absorb. This is reflected strongly in all of the commentaries – 'leaving no stone unturned' is a sound bite which certainly rings true. SW relates a powerful story of how careful identification and implementation of the enablers that needed to be in place resulted in outstanding and sustained levels of performance for years after. DS describes how at the Australian Institute of Sport an environment had been carefully constructed for the athletes in which every detail had been considered and accommodated; the athletes had access to the latest and best enablers available. JG believes that perhaps the most important aspect of delivering top performance is an awareness that 'details really do matter'.

SW and GH rightly emphasise the importance of having people with the right skills in the right positions but they also recognise that this is not where leadership ends. What is clearly apparent relates to my premise in Part 3.4 that top performance leaders cannot motivate these people; their crucial role is to provide the conditions where people feel intrinsically motivated. Even top performers will not remain motivated indefinitely if the conditions are not conducive to them keeping themselves motivated. Leaders must create conditions in which people can thrive. Helping to instil a sense of belonging in people emerges as particularly important in several of the commentaries as underpinning the self-motivation that people thrive on. JP's reference to discretionary effort reminds us that people choose how much effort they will put in and self-motivation lies at its core. And DS's vivid recall of his coach's mantra that 'I can't swim the race for you' is powerful testimony to the responsibility, accountability and top performance that people can achieve if the leader pays careful attention to the environment s/he has created.

The environment leaders create is inevitably dynamic and their role is to continually enhance and optimise it through their leadership. The concept of *real* leadership particularly resonated with JG, GH and SW in this regard. JG's story of the senior physician who got his team together figures again here because this leader was *real* by involving them in discussions around expectations when it would have been very easy to follow the conventional *safe* option of just telling them what to do. SW relates the story of the visionary, inspiring and compelling *real* leader she had worked alongside and the impact he had on leading change and delivering the vision. GH has first-hand experience of observing *safe* leaders lose their way, and he has also witnessed *real* leaders in action in the form of assuming absolute responsibility to role model the behaviours and values that represent their non-negotiables. GH continues by making a strong link between *real* and sustainable leadership, and particularly *real* leaders' ability to self-actualise. DS refers to his coach as being 'extremely comfortable in himself' and also having an ego that allowed his swimmers to explore different options with input from other people. These represent a self-belief and humility respectively that are important building blocks in sustainable leadership.

An aspect of top performance leadership that was a common theme in the commentaries and which is implicit throughout the book's content is that of learning and feedback. JP, in particular, is strong on the role of learning through constant review and debriefing in this process and this sentiment is echoed by JG. This is perhaps not surprising given that both come from worlds in which they have operated 'at the edges of performance' where lives are at stake. However, feedback figures prominently in the other commentaries as well. Therefore, it is clear that whatever the performance context and setting, top performance leaders are always looking for ways to improve all aspects of performance, the environment and themselves.

Finally, I want to draw your attention to the very essence of top performance leadership and it exists in the commentaries of GH and JP. In different ways, they imply that leaders do not have to know too much about the performance sector they are operating in to oversee the delivery of top performance, and also, they do not have to be the best performers. GH describes how, despite his lack of medical, aviation or direct social sector experience, his leadership is transforming his organisation. JP talks about how 'most squadron commanders will not be the best pilot in that room'. The essence of top performance leadership is that you do not have to know the most or be the best. Top performance leaders ensure that the definition of performance is crystal clear. They then create and optimise the conditions in which their people can thrive and become top performers. And then they lead accordingly.

Index